THE FEAST OF EROS

A MODERN ADAPTATION OF PLATO'S SYMPOSIUM

PLATO

Translated by

FILIBOOKS TRANSLATION

FILIBOOKS.COM

Cover by: Filibooks Covers

Published by: Filibooks Classics

Filibooks ApS

info@filibooks.com

CVR: 37100161

Paperback ISBN: 978-87-94559-31-7
Ebook ISBN: 978-87-94559-32-4

CONTENTS

INTRODUCTION

Plato's "Συμπόσιον", commonly rendered in English as "Symposium" but here presented as "The Feast of Eros," stands as a cornerstone of Western philosophy. This new translation aims to breathe fresh life into this ancient text, capturing its intellectual rigor, dramatic flair, and timeless insights into the nature of love and human desire.

Set against the backdrop of an Athenian drinking party, this dialogue transcends its historical context to probe universal questions about love, beauty, and the human condition. Plato's genius lies in his ability to transmute the convivial atmosphere of a banquet into a crucible for philosophical inquiry, blending intellectual discourse with dramatic tension and subtle humor.

The Historical and Cultural Context

To fully appreciate "The Feast of Eros," one must understand its historical and cultural context. The dialogue is set in 416 BCE, a time of both greatness and impending doom for Athens. The city-state was at the height of its power, yet on the brink of the disastrous Sicilian Expedition that would mark the beginning of its decline. This setting provides a poignant backdrop for a discussion on the nature of love and beauty, as the characters unknowingly stand at the twilight of their civilization's golden age.

The symposium itself was a crucial institution in ancient Greek culture. These drinking parties were not mere occasions for revelry, but served as venues for intellectual discourse, political networking, and artistic performance. By setting his philosophical exploration within this context, Plato bridges the gap between the lofty realm of ideas and the earthy reality of human experience.

Structure and Philosophical Progression

The structure of the dialogue—a series of speeches on love, each building upon and challenging the last—mirrors the Platonic conception of philosophical progress. As the night unfolds, we witness an ascent from more corporeal understandings of love to increasingly abstract and sophisticated conceptualizations. This progression culminates in Socrates' recounting of Diotima's teachings, which presents love as a ladder leading to the apprehension of absolute beauty.

Each speaker serves as a unique prism, refracting the concept of love:

1. Phaedrus views love through the lens of civic virtue and heroic mythology. His speech sets the stage by linking love to noble deeds and societal benefit.
2. Pausanias introduces moral complexity, distinguishing between base and noble forms of love. This nuanced view challenges the simplistic notion of love as universally good.
3. Eryximachus, the physician, expands love into a cosmic principle of harmony. His scientific perspective broadens the concept beyond human relationships to encompass all of nature.
4. Aristophanes offers a poignant origin myth that casts love as a quest for wholeness. His comedic yet touching tale of

split humans searching for their other halves has captivated readers for millennia.

5. Agathon, the tragedian, praises love with poetic flourish, attributing to it all virtues. His speech represents the height of rhetorical skill, setting the stage for Socrates' deconstruction.

6. Socrates, via Diotima, elevates love to a philosophical method for apprehending the Forms. This speech forms the philosophical core of the dialogue, presenting Plato's mature theory of love and its relation to the pursuit of wisdom.

7. Alcibiades crashes the party to provide a raw, personal account of philosophical eros embodied in Socrates. His speech serves as both a climax and a counterpoint, grounding the preceding abstract discussions in lived experience.

This progression is not merely a literary device but a philosophical argument in itself, suggesting that understanding love requires synthesizing multiple perspectives, from the physical to the metaphysical, the personal to the universal.

Revolutionary Concept of Love

Plato's treatment of love in "The Feast of Eros" is revolutionary in its scope and depth. In his rendering, love is not merely a personal emotion or physical attraction, but a fundamental force driving all human striving. It is the root of philosophy (love of wisdom), the basis of ethics (love of the good), and the path to enlightenment (love of the beautiful).

By expanding the concept of love to encompass all forms of desire and aspiration, Plato transforms it from a subject of poetry and romance into a central philosophical principle. Love, in this view, becomes the motivating force behind all human achievement, from artistic creation to scientific discovery to political reform.

Moreover, Plato presents love as a kind of "divine madness," a state that takes us beyond our ordinary selves and connects us to something greater. This idea challenges the common perception of philosophy as a purely rational endeavor, suggesting instead that true wisdom requires a kind of inspired passion.

The Platonic conception of love as presented in this dialogue has had a profound influence on Western thought, shaping ideas about romance, spirituality, and the nature of the good life for over two millennia.

Literary Artistry and Philosophical Method

This translation strives to capture the multifaceted nature of Plato's prose, conveying not only the philosophical content but also the literary artistry, the subtle humor, and the dramatic tension that make "The Feast of Eros" a masterpiece of both ideas and storytelling.

Plato's use of the dialogue form is not merely a stylistic choice, but an essential part of his philosophical method. By presenting multiple viewpoints and allowing them to clash and intermingle, he encourages readers to engage actively with the ideas, rather than passively receiving doctrine. The dialogue form also allows Plato to explore the limitations of language and the written word in conveying philosophical truth, a theme he returns to in many of his works.

Particular attention has been paid to preserving the distinct voices of each speaker, from the flowery rhetoric of Agathon to the earthy humor of Aristophanes and the penetrating logic of Socrates. These varied styles not only add to the literary richness of the text but also reflect different modes of thinking about love and reality.

Key Concepts and Terms

The rendering of key terms presents both a challenge and an opportunity for deeper understanding. The Greek 'eros,' for instance, encompasses a range of meanings not fully captured by the English 'love.' It implies a passionate, often physical desire that drives the lover towards the beloved. This conception of love as a driving force, rather than merely a feeling, is crucial to understanding Plato's philosophical argument.

Similarly, 'kalos,' translated variously as 'beautiful' and 'noble,' unites aesthetic and moral excellence in a way that challenges modern categorical distinctions. For the ancient Greeks, and for Plato in particular, beauty was not merely a matter of appearance but was intimately connected with goodness and truth.

Other key concepts that receive extensive treatment in the dialogue include:

- The relationship between lover and beloved, and the moral dynamics of Greek pederasty
- The nature of the soul and its journey towards wisdom
- The theory of Forms, particularly as it relates to the Form of Beauty
- The role of poetry and rhetoric in conveying truth
- The figure of Socrates as the ideal philosopher and lover of wisdom

The Speech of Alcibiades: A Dramatic Climax

Alcibiades' speech serves as both climax and counterpoint to the preceding philosophical discussions. His unvarnished account of his relationship with Socrates provides a concrete illustration of philosophical eros in action, while also offering a unique portrait of Socrates as seen through the eyes of one who both loved and felt spurned by him.

This speech is crucial for several reasons:

1. It grounds the lofty philosophical discussions in the messy reality of human relationships, highlighting the tension between the ideal and the real that runs throughout the dialogue.

2. It provides insight into the character of Socrates, presenting him as a living embodiment of the philosophical ideals discussed earlier.
3. It explores the transformative power of philosophical love, showing how Socrates' influence could profoundly affect those around him.
4. It serves as a cautionary tale, illustrating the dangers of misunderstanding or misapplying the concepts of philosophical eros.

The inclusion of this speech, with its raw emotion and personal detail, demonstrates Plato's commitment to exploring love not just as an abstract concept, but as a lived experience.

Relevance and Enduring Impact

"The Feast of Eros" is not merely an exposition of ancient ideas, but a living philosophical drama that continues to provoke thought and debate. It challenges readers to consider fundamental questions: What is the nature of love? How does desire relate to virtue? What is the relationship between the physical and the spiritual? How can we ascend from particular beauties to universal Beauty itself?

The dialogue's exploration of love as a path to higher understanding has influenced fields far beyond philosophy, shaping Western literature, psychology, and spirituality. Its impact can be seen in everything from courtly love poetry to Freudian psychoanalysis to contemporary self-help literature.

Moreover, the questions it raises about the nature of desire, the quest for meaning, and the possibility of transcendence remain as relevant today as they were in Plato's time. In an age often characterized by superficial relationships and material pursuits, "The Feast of Eros" offers a compelling vision of love as a transformative force that can lead us to greater wisdom and virtue.

Conclusion

As you engage with this text, prepare to be challenged, amused, and perhaps transformed. For in grappling with Plato's ideas, we are not simply studying an ancient philosopher, but participating in an ongoing conversation about the nature of love, the pursuit of wisdom, and the essence of human experience.

"The Feast of Eros" invites us not just to think about love, but to fall in love with thinking itself. It challenges us to see love not as a mere emotion or physical attraction, but as a fundamental force that can elevate us from the mundane to the divine. In doing so, it offers not just a philosophy of love, but a love of philosophy—a vision of intellectual and spiritual pursuit as the highest form of human endeavor.

As you read, allow yourself to be drawn into the world of the dialogue, to wrestle with its ideas, to question your own assumptions about love and desire. For it is in this active engagement, this philosophical eros, that the true power of Plato's masterpiece lies. May this new translation serve as a gateway to that transformative experience, inviting a new generation of readers to join in the eternal feast of ideas that is "The Feast of Eros."

STEPHANUS PAGINATION (CROSS-REFERENCING)

The Stephanus pagination system, crucial for engaging with Plato's works, provides a universal referencing method for Platonic dialogues. Named after 16th-century printer Henricus Stephanus (Henri Estienne), it enables precise citation across diverse translations and editions.

Stephanus's 1578 publication of Plato's works introduced an innovative layout, sectioning the text and marking subsections with letters (a-e) on each page. Modern editions maintain these divisions, usually in the margins.

"The Feast of Eros 172a" directs readers to the dialogue's opening, while "The Feast of Eros 223d" indicates its conclusion. For cross-referencing with older translations, simply substitute "Symposium" for "The Feast of Eros" in citations. This standardization facilitates textual analysis and scholarly discourse across linguistic and temporal boundaries.

This translation integrates Stephanus numbers throughout, allowing seamless comparison with other translations and the original Greek. This pagination aids comparative study and ensures the enduring accessibility of Plato's insights, transcending language barriers and centuries of interpretation.

By employing this system, readers can navigate Plato's thought with precision, tracing the development of arguments across different sections.

THE FEAST OF EROS

[172A] "I believe I'm well-prepared to answer your questions," Apollodorus began. "Just the other day, I was making my way up to the city from my home in Phalerum when an acquaintance spotted me from behind and called out playfully, 'Hey, Phalerian! Apollodorus! Won't you wait up?'

I stopped and waited for him to catch up. 'Apollodorus,' he said, 'I've been looking for you. I wanted to hear all about the gathering at Agathon's house [172b] – you know, the one with Socrates, Alcibiades, and the others. I'm particularly curious about the speeches on love they gave. Someone else told me about it – he heard it from Phoenix, Philip's son – and mentioned that you knew about it too. But he couldn't give me any clear details. You're the best person to report on your friend's words. But first,' he added, 'tell me, were you there yourself or not?'

'Your informant,' I replied, 'must have been quite vague indeed [172c] if you think this gathering was so recent that I could have attended.'

'That's what I thought,' he said.

'How could that be, Glaucon?' I asked. 'Don't you know that Agathon hasn't been in Athens for many years? It's been less than three years since I began to spend time with Socrates and made it my daily priority to know what he says and does. Before that, I was just running around aimlessly, thinking I was doing something important when I was really more miserable than anyone – not unlike you now, thinking that anything is more worthwhile than philosophy.'

[173a] 'Don't mock me,' he said. 'Just tell me when this gathering took place.'

'We were still boys,' I answered. 'It was when Agathon won the prize with his first tragedy, the day after he and his chorus celebrated the victory.'

'Oh, that was ages ago,' he said. 'But who told you about it? Was it Socrates himself?'

[173b] 'Good heavens, no,' I said. 'It was the same person who told Phoenix – Aristodemus, a little fellow from Cydathenaeum who always went barefoot. He was there at the gathering, being one of Socrates' most devoted admirers at the time, I believe. However, I've also checked some points with Socrates since then, and he confirmed Aristodemus' account.'

'Well then,' Glaucon said, 'why don't you tell me about it? The road to town is perfect for talking and listening as we walk.'

So, as we made our way along, we discussed it, which is why, as I said at the beginning, I'm not unprepared. [173c] If you want me to go through it all again, that's what I'll do. I must say, when it comes to philosophical discussions, whether I'm speaking myself or listening to others, I find them incredibly enjoyable, quite apart from thinking they're beneficial. But when I hear other kinds of talk, especially the sort you wealthy businessmen engage in, it bores me to tears, and I feel sorry for you and your friends because you think you're achieving something when you're really accomplishing nothing. [173d] Perhaps you, in turn, think I'm the unfortunate one, and I suspect you're right in thinking so. But I don't just think you're unfortunate – I know it for a fact."

"You never change, Apollodorus," his companion replied. "You're always putting yourself and everyone else down. You seem to think everyone's miserable except Socrates, yourself included. I don't know how you got this reputation for being 'soft,' because your words are always so harsh – to yourself and to everyone else, except Socrates."

[173e] "My dear friend," Apollodorus retorted, "isn't it obvious that holding such opinions about myself and all of you is precisely what makes me mad and delusional?"

"It's not worth arguing about this now, Apollodorus," his friend said. "Just do as we asked and tell us about the speeches."

"All right, then. They went something like this – but perhaps [174a] I should try to recount it from the beginning, just as Aristodemus did for me[1].

Aristodemus said that he met Socrates, freshly bathed and wearing sandals, both unusual for him. Aristodemus asked where he was going, looking so dapper.

Socrates replied that he was headed to dinner at Agathon's house. 'I avoided yesterday's victory celebration,' he explained, 'fearing the crowd. But I promised to come today. So I've made myself presentable to match my handsome host. But what about you?' he asked. [174b] 'How would you like to come to dinner uninvited?'

Aristodemus said he'd do whatever Socrates suggested.

'Come along then,' Socrates said, 'and we'll disprove the proverb by showing that "Good men go uninvited to good men's feasts". Homer, you see, not only disproved this proverb but positively insulted it. He made Agamemnon an exceptionally good warrior, and Menelaus a 'feeble spearman.' [174c] Yet when Agamemnon was sacrificing and feasting, he had Menelaus come uninvited, the inferior man to the better man's table.'

Aristodemus said he was worried about this, saying, 'I'm afraid I'm more like Homer's uninvited guest – not as you describe, Socrates, but more like a worthless fellow turning up uninvited at a wise man's table. What will you say to excuse me? Because I won't admit to coming uninvited – I'll say you invited me.'

[174d] 'As two go together,' Socrates replied, quoting Homer, 'one can think ahead of the other. We'll decide what to say as we go. Let's be off.'

With such banter, Aristodemus said, they set out. But as they walked, Socrates began to fall behind, lost in thought. When Aristodemus waited, Socrates told him to go on ahead.

When Aristodemus arrived at Agathon's house, [174e] he found the door open and had an awkward moment. A servant immediately led him to where the others were reclining, about to begin dinner. Agathon, seeing him, called out, 'Aristodemus! Welcome! Come join us for dinner. If you're here for any other reason, we can discuss it later. I was looking for you yesterday to invite you, but couldn't find you. But where's Socrates?'

Aristodemus turned around, but Socrates was nowhere to be seen. He explained that he had come with Socrates, invited by him to dinner.

'That was good of you,' said Agathon, 'but where is he?'

[175a] "He was right behind me just now," Apollodorus continued. "I'm surprised he's not here yet."

"Boy," Agathon called out, "go look for Socrates and bring him in. And you, Aristodemus, come lie down next to Eryximachus."

As one servant was washing Aristodemus' feet so he could recline, another came with news: "Socrates has wandered off to the neighbors' porch. He's just standing there, and he won't come in despite my calls."

"How odd," remarked Agathon. "Go call him again and don't take no for an answer."

[175b] But Aristodemus interjected, "No, no, leave him be. It's a habit of his. Sometimes he just wanders off and stands wherever he happens to be. He'll be here shortly, I'm sure. Don't disturb him, just let him be."

"Very well, if you think so," Agathon conceded. "Now, boys, serve the rest of us. Feel free to bring whatever you like, as you always do when there's no one supervising—which I never do. So today, imagine that I and these other guests have been invited to dinner by you. Take good care of us, and we'll sing your praises."

They began their meal, but Socrates was still absent. Agathon repeatedly suggested sending for him, but Aristodemus wouldn't allow it. [175c] Finally, Socrates arrived, having spent less time than usual in his contemplative state, just as they were midway through dinner.

Agathon, who happened to be reclining alone at the end of the table, called out, "Socrates, come lie down next to me. I want to absorb some of that wisdom you've just acquired standing in the doorway. You must have found what you were looking for, or you wouldn't have moved."

Socrates sat down and replied with a touch of irony, "Wouldn't it be wonderful, Agathon, if wisdom could flow from the fuller to the emptier among us when we touch, [175d] like water flowing through wool from a full cup to an empty one? If that's how wisdom works, I greatly value my place beside you. I expect to be filled with your abundant and exquisite wisdom. Mine is rather paltry and question-able, like a dream, while yours is brilliant and bursting with potential. Why, just the other day it shone forth from your youthful mind, radi-ating before more than thirty thousand Greek witnesses."

[175e] "You're a tease, Socrates," Agathon retorted. "We'll soon put our respective wisdom to the test, with Dionysus as our judge. But for now, focus on your dinner."

After Socrates had reclined and dined, and the others had finished their meal, they poured libations, sang hymns to the god, and performed the other customary rites. Then they turned their attention to drinking. [176a] Pausanias opened the discussion:

"Well, gentlemen, how can we drink most comfortably? I must say, I'm in quite a state from yesterday's overindulgence and could use some recovery—I suspect many of you feel the same, as you were here yesterday. So, let's consider how we might drink most easily."

Aristophanes chimed in, "That's a good point, Pausanias. We should definitely arrange for some moderation in our drinking. I'm one of those who got thoroughly soaked yesterday."

Hearing this, Eryximachus, son of Acumenus, said, "Well put, both of you. But I'd like to hear from one more person: Agathon, how do you feel about drinking heartily tonight?"

[176b] "Not at all up to it, I'm afraid," Agathon replied.

"This is fortunate for us," Eryximachus declared, "I mean for myself, Aristodemus, Phaedrus, and the others, if you heavy drinkers are giving it a rest tonight. We're always lightweights when it comes to drinking. I exclude Socrates, of course; he's capable of either drinking or not, so he'll be fine with whatever we decide. Now, since it seems no one here is eager to drink heavily, perhaps I might be less unwelcome if I speak some truths about intoxication. [176c] My medical training has made it clear to me how harmful drunkenness is to people. I'm personally reluctant to overindulge, and I wouldn't advise it to others, especially when they're still hungover from the day before."

"As usual, Eryximachus," interjected Phaedrus of Myrrhinus, "I defer to you, especially in matters of medicine. And if they're wise, the others will do the same."

[176d] Hearing this, they all agreed not to make this gathering about getting drunk, but to drink only for pleasure.

"Well then," said Eryximachus, "since we've decided that each should drink as much as he wishes, with no compulsion, I propose we send away the flute-girl who just came in. Let her play for herself or for the women in the house, if she likes. Tonight, let's entertain each other with conversation. And if you're agreeable, I'd like to suggest a topic."

[177a] Apollodorus continued his account: "They all agreed, urging Eryximachus to proceed with his proposal. Eryximachus then began, 'I shall start, as Euripides might say in his Melanippe, with a tale not my own, but that of our friend Phaedrus here. Phaedrus often complains to me, saying, "Isn't it strange, Eryximachus, that while poets have composed hymns and paeans to other gods, not one of them has ever written an encomium to Love, ancient and powerful as he is? [177b] Look at the worthy sophists: they write elaborate praises of Heracles and others – Prodicus, for instance, has done so admirably. Even more surprisingly, I once came across a book by a learned man singing the praises of salt and its usefulness. Indeed, you can find eulogies on all manner of trivial things. [177c] Yet, despite all this attention to such matters, not a single person, to this very day, has attempted to compose a proper hymn to Love. Such a

great god, so utterly neglected!" I must say, I think Phaedrus has a point.

'Therefore, I wish to make amends to Love and offer my contribution. Moreover, it seems fitting for us, gathered here, to honor this god. If you agree, we could spend our time in discourse. I propose that each of us, from left to right, deliver the finest eulogy to Love that we can muster. Phaedrus should begin, as he's both the originator of this idea and occupies the first place.'

[177d] Socrates chimed in, 'No one will vote against your proposal, Eryximachus. I certainly won't object, claiming as I do to be an expert in matters of love. Neither will Agathon and Pausanias, nor Aristophanes, whose entire life revolves around Dionysus and Aphrodite. In fact, no one present would disagree. [177e] However, it's not quite fair to those of us seated last. If our predecessors speak well and thoroughly, we'll have little left to say. But let Phaedrus begin with good fortune, and let him sing Love's praises.'

Everyone present echoed Socrates' sentiments and urged Phaedrus to begin. [178a] Phaedrus began his speech by declaring Love to be a great and wondrous god, revered by both mortals and immortals alike. He emphasized Love's ancient origins, stating, 'To be among the oldest of the gods is a mark of honor. And we have proof of Love's primeval nature: neither prose writer nor poet has ever claimed Love had parents. [178b] Hesiod tells us that first came Chaos, and then:

> *"Broad-bosomed Earth, ever-secure seat of all,*
> *And Love..."*

Acusilaus agrees with Hesiod that after Chaos came Earth and Love. Parmenides speaks of Love's genesis thus:

> *"First of all the gods, she devised Love."*

[178c] So, from many sources, we hear that Love is among the most ancient of gods. And being so old, Love is the source of our greatest blessings. I can think of no greater good for a young person

than a noble lover, and for a lover, than a worthy beloved. What should guide humans throughout life, if they are to live well, is not family, nor honors, nor wealth, nor any other thing, so much as love. [178d] What do I mean by this? I speak of the sense of shame in disgraceful acts and the aspiration to honor in noble ones. Without these, neither city nor individual can achieve anything great or fine.

I contend that a man in love, if caught doing something shameful or enduring something degrading without defending himself, would feel less pain at being seen by his father, his companions, or anyone else than by his beloved. [178e] We observe the same in the beloved, who is especially ashamed before his lover when caught in some disgraceful situation. If we could somehow create a city or an army composed of lovers and their beloveds, we could not find a better foundation for society than this mutual striving to avoid shame and seek honor in each other's eyes. [179a] Such men, fighting side by side, even if few in number, could conquer the world, so to speak.

A lover would rather be seen by all others deserting his post or throwing away his weapons than by his beloved, and would choose death many times over before that. As for abandoning the beloved or failing to help in danger – no one is so base that Love itself could not inspire him to valor, making him equal to the bravest by nature. As Homer says, the god 'breathes might' into some heroes; so Love inspires lovers.

[179b] Moreover, only lovers are willing to die for another. This is true not only of men but of women also. Alcestis, daughter of Pelias, provides ample testimony to this argument for the Greeks. She alone was willing to die for her husband, though he had both a father and mother living. Her love so far exceeded theirs [179c] that she made them seem strangers to their son, related in name only. When she did this, her deed appeared so noble in the eyes of gods and men that, among the many who have done great and beautiful deeds, she is one of the very few to whom the gods have granted the privilege of returning alive from Hades. So even the gods honor devotion and virtue in love above all.

[179d] They sent Orpheus, son of Oeagrus, back from Hades

empty-handed. They showed him only a phantom of the wife he came to retrieve, not granting him the real woman, for they thought him soft, being a lyre-player, lacking the courage to die for love as Alcestis had done. Instead, he contrived to enter Hades alive. For this, they punished him, causing his death at the hands of women.

[179e] Achilles, son of Thetis, on the other hand, they honored and sent to the Isles of the Blest. He had learned from his mother that he would die if he killed Hector, but could return home and live to a ripe old age if he did not. Yet he dared to choose to aid his lover Patroclus, to avenge him, and to die not only for him but after him. [180a] The gods were so impressed that they gave him exceptional honor, because he valued his lover so highly.

Aeschylus is mistaken when he claims that Achilles was in love with Patroclus. Achilles was far more beautiful, not only compared to Patroclus but to all heroes. He was beardless and much younger, as Homer tells us. In truth, the gods hold this virtue of love in the highest esteem, [180b] yet they marvel even more, admire, and bestow their blessings when the beloved cherishes his lover, rather than when the lover dotes on his beloved. For the lover has something divine about him—he is inspired. This is why they honored Achilles more than Alcestis, sending him to the Isles of the Blessed.

Thus, I declare that Love is the most ancient, most honored, and most powerful of the gods in guiding humans toward virtue and happiness, both in life and after death.

[180c] Phaedrus, it was said, gave a speech along these lines. After him, there were others whose words I cannot quite recall. Passing over these, I will relate Pausanias's speech. He began by saying, "Phaedrus, I believe our task has not been well defined. We have been instructed to simply praise Love, but this is too simplistic. If Love were singular, it would be fitting, but this is not the case. Since there is more than one kind of Love, it would be more appropriate to first specify which Love we should praise. [180d] I will attempt to rectify this by first describing which Love should be praised, and then offering praise worthy of the god.

We all know that Aphrodite is inseparable from Love. If there were only one Aphrodite, there would be only one Love. But since there are two goddesses, there must necessarily be two Loves. How can we deny that there are two goddesses? One is older, the motherless daughter of Heaven, whom we call Heavenly Aphrodite (Aphrodite Urania). The other is younger, daughter of Zeus and Dione, [180e] whom we call Common Aphrodite (Aphrodite Pandemos). It follows that the Love associated with the latter should be called Common Love, and the other, Heavenly Love.

While we should praise all gods, we must attempt to distinguish the nature of each. Every action is neutral in itself—neither noble nor base. [181a] Take what we are doing now: drinking, singing, or conversing. None of these acts is inherently noble; it becomes so only in the manner of its execution. When done well and rightly, it becomes noble; when done poorly, it becomes base. The same applies to love and Love: not every form is noble or praiseworthy, but only that which inspires us to love nobly.

The Love of Common Aphrodite is truly common, acting randomly. [181b] This is the love that inferior people feel. Such people love women as much as boys, and they love bodies more than souls. They seek the least intelligent partners, focusing only on the physical act and disregarding whether their actions are noble or not. Consequently, they act without discrimination, doing good or bad indiscriminately. This love comes from the goddess who is both younger and of mixed female and male parentage in her origin.

[181c] But the Love of Heavenly Aphrodite springs from a goddess who, firstly, has no female element but only male—hence this is the love of boys—and secondly, is older and free from wanton violence. Those inspired by this love are drawn to what is naturally stronger and more intelligent. One can recognize those genuinely motivated by this love even among pederasts: [181d] they do not love boys, but rather those who have begun to develop intellect, which occurs around the time of growing their first beard. Those who begin to love at this stage are prepared, I believe, to be together for life and share their lives in common. They do not intend to deceive, taking advantage of a youth's foolishness, only to laugh and run off to another.

There ought to be a law forbidding the love of young boys, [181e] so that much effort is not wasted on an uncertain outcome. For it is unclear how a boy will turn out in terms of vice or virtue, in both body and soul. Good men impose this law upon themselves willingly, but it should also be imposed on common lovers, just as we prohibit them, as far as possible, from loving freeborn women. [182a]

These are the ones who have brought reproach upon love, leading some to dare say that it is shameful to gratify lovers. They say this with these common lovers in mind, seeing their impropriety and injustice, for surely nothing done with propriety and according to custom would justly invite reproach.

Indeed, the law concerning love in other cities is easy to understand, as it is simply defined. But here and in Sparta, it is complex. [182b] In Elis and Boeotia, and where people are not skilled in speaking, it is simply decreed that gratifying lovers is noble, and no one, young or old, would say it is shameful. This, I believe, is to save themselves the trouble of trying to persuade the young with arguments, as they are incapable of speaking eloquently. But in Ionia and many other places ruled by barbarians, it is considered shameful. Among barbarians, due to their tyrannical governments, this and the love of wisdom and athletics are considered shameful. [182c] For I imagine it is not advantageous for their rulers that great ideas should arise in their subjects, nor strong friendships and partnerships, which love, above all else, tends to produce.

Our tyrants here learned this from experience: Aristogeiton's love and Harmodius's friendship, once it became steadfast, overthrew their rule. Thus, where the law holds it shameful to gratify lovers, [182d] this is due to the vice of the lawmakers—the rulers' greed and the subjects' cowardice. Where it is considered simply noble, it is due to the mental laziness of the lawmakers. But our law is far nobler, though as I said, not easy to understand.

Consider how it's deemed nobler to love openly than in secret, especially when the beloved is of the noblest and finest character, even if they may not be the most physically attractive. Observe how a lover receives universal encouragement, not as though engaged in something shameful. [182e] Society applauds their success and scorns their failure, granting them extraordinary license to pursue their goal – actions that, in any other context, would invite the harshest criticism.

[183a] Imagine if someone, in pursuit of wealth, political office, or any other ambition, were to behave as lovers do: making impassioned pleas, swearing fervent oaths, sleeping on doorsteps, and willingly submitting to forms of servitude that even a slave would balk at. Such a person would be derided by friends and foes alike, [183b] accused of flattery and lack of self-respect. Yet when a lover does these very things, it's seen as charming. Custom not only permits but celebrates such behavior as if it were the noblest pursuit imaginable.

Most astonishing of all, it's commonly believed that the gods forgive lovers who break their oaths, for they say there's no such thing as a "lover's oath." [183c] Thus, both divine and human law grant the lover total freedom, as our local custom affirms.

One might conclude from this that our city holds love and the formation of romantic attachments in the highest regard. But then consider: fathers appoint guardians to prevent their sons from speaking with suitors, friends and peers criticize any such interactions they witness, [183d] and elders neither intervene nor rebuke this criticism as misguided. Observing these contradictions, one might instead deduce that such practices are considered utterly disgraceful here.

The truth, I believe, is this: the matter is not simple. As I said at the outset, no action is inherently noble or shameful; it's the manner of its execution that determines its nature. To gratify a base person basely is shameful, while to gratify a noble person nobly is admirable. The base lover is the common sort, more enamored with the body than the soul. [183e] Such love is fleeting, for it's founded on that which is itself impermanent. When the bloom of youth fades, this lover "flits away," leaving behind nothing but broken promises and tarnished reputations. In contrast, the lover of noble character remains constant throughout life, having bonded with that which endures.

[184a] Our custom seeks to thoroughly test these lovers, encouraging us to yield to some while fleeing from others. It urges the pursuit and the flight, setting up a contest to determine which category both the lover and the beloved fall into. This is why we consider it shameful to yield too quickly – time is needed for proper assessment. It's also deemed disgraceful to be won over by money or political influence, [184b] whether by succumbing to ill-treatment and intimidation or by being unable to resist the allure of wealth and power. None of these foundations are stable or lasting, and they're incapable of fostering genuine friendship.

According to our custom, there remains only one honorable path for the beloved to gratify their lover. Just as we said earlier that any form of willing servitude to one's beloved is not considered flattery or worthy of reproach, [184c] so too is there one form of voluntary servitude that is free from shame: that which is done in pursuit of virtue. Our tradition holds that if someone chooses to serve another, believing that through them they will improve in wisdom or in any other aspect of virtue, this willing servitude is neither shameful nor sycophantic.

These two principles – the one concerning love between men and the one concerning the pursuit of wisdom and virtue – must align if the gratification of a lover by their beloved is to be truly noble. [184d] When lover and beloved come together, each guided by their respective principle – the lover justly serving the beloved who has gratified him, and the beloved justly assisting the one who is making him wise and good – with one able to contribute to the other's intellectual and moral growth, and the other seeking education and wisdom, [184e] only then, when these conditions converge, is it noble for the beloved to gratify the lover. Under no other circumstances is this the case. In this context, even to be deceived is no disgrace, while in all other cases, it brings shame whether one is deceived or not.

[185a] For if someone gratifies a lover believing them to be wealthy, only to discover they are poor and no money is forthcoming, it's no less shameful. Such a person has revealed their true nature – willing to do anything for anyone for the sake of money, which is

ignoble. Conversely, if someone gratifies a lover believing them to be good and expecting to become better through their friendship, only to find that the lover is base and lacking in virtue, the deception is still honorable. [185b] For they have demonstrated that, for the sake of virtue and self-improvement, they would eagerly do anything for anyone – and this is the noblest of all motivations. Thus, to gratify another for the sake of virtue is always honorable.

This is the love inspired by the heavenly Aphrodite – a celestial and invaluable force for both cities and individuals, compelling both lover and beloved to devote themselves to cultivating virtue. [185c] All other forms of love belong to the common Aphrodite. This, Phaedrus, is my impromptu contribution on the subject of Love.

When Pausanias paused – for I must match these clever speakers in their balanced phrases – Aristodemus reported that it was Aristophanes' turn to speak. However, whether from overeating or some other cause, he had an attack of hiccups and was unable to proceed. He turned to the physician Eryximachus, who was reclining on the couch below him, and said, [185d] "Eryximachus, it's only fair that you either cure my hiccups or speak in my place until they pass."

Eryximachus replied, "I shall do both. I'll speak in your turn, and you in mine once you've recovered. While I'm speaking, if you hold your breath for a long time, your hiccups should cease. If not, gargle with some water. [185e] If they're particularly stubborn, take something to tickle your nose and sneeze. Do this once or twice, and no matter how severe, they will stop."

"Begin your speech at once," said Aristophanes. "I'll follow your instructions."

[186a] Eryximachus began, "It seems to me that since Pausanias has made a fine start but failed to bring his argument to a satisfactory conclusion, I must attempt to complete it. The notion of Love's dual nature is, I believe, a sound distinction. However, I would argue that Love's influence extends far beyond the realm of human souls and their attraction to beauty. As a physician, I have observed that Love permeates all of existence—the bodies of all living creatures, the plants that grow from the earth, and indeed, all things that are. [186b]

Our art of medicine has revealed to me the profound and wondrous ways in which this god exerts his power over both mortal and divine affairs.

Let me begin with medicine, to pay homage to my profession. The very nature of our bodies embodies this duality of Love. Health and sickness are universally acknowledged as distinct and dissimilar states, and it is the nature of dissimilar things to desire and love what is unlike them. Thus, the love that exists in a healthy body differs from that in a diseased one. [186c] Just as Pausanias spoke of the nobility in gratifying good men and the shame in pandering to the intemperate, so too in our bodies: it is right and proper to indulge the good and healthy elements, which is the essence of medicine, while it is shameful and must be denied to the bad and sickly parts. The true physician is one who can distinguish between these noble and base loves within the body.

[186d] In essence, medicine is the knowledge of the body's loves in relation to repletion and evacuation. The most skilled physician is one who can not only discern between good and bad loves but can also effect a change, replacing one love with another. He must be able to instill love where it is absent and remove it where it is unwanted. His craft lies in making the most hostile elements within the body become friendly and love one another. [186e] The most inimical elements are, of course, the opposites: hot and cold, bitter and sweet, wet and dry. It was our ancestor Asclepius who, by infusing love and harmony into these opposites, established our art, as the poets claim and I firmly believe.

[187a] Thus, medicine in its entirety is guided by this god, as are gymnastics and agriculture. Music, too, as anyone with even a modicum of attention can see, operates on the same principles. This is perhaps what Heraclitus[2] intended to convey, though his words are somewhat obscure. He speaks of unity, disagreeing with itself yet in agreement, like the tension in a bow or a lyre. Now, it's quite illogical to speak of harmony as disagreeing with itself or as arising from elements that are still in discord. [187b] What he likely meant was that harmony is created from elements that once differed—high and low

notes—but have since been brought into agreement by the art of music.

For indeed, harmony cannot arise from high and low notes that are still at variance. Harmony is agreement, and agreement cannot come from disagreement as long as disagreement persists. Similarly, rhythm is born from the fast and the slow, which were once at odds but later reconciled. [187c] In both cases, it is music that, like medicine, brings about this reconciliation, instilling mutual love and accord. Thus, music is the science of love as it pertains to harmony and rhythm.

In the basic composition of harmony and rhythm, it is not difficult to discern these elements of love, and the dual nature of love is not yet apparent. But when it comes to applying rhythm and harmony in relation to humans—whether in composition, which we call lyric poetry, or in the correct use of composed melodies and measures, which we term education—then the task becomes challenging and requires a skilled craftsman. [187d] For here again we encounter the same principle: we must gratify and preserve the love of orderly men, and of those who, though not yet orderly, might become so. This is the noble, heavenly love, the love of the heavenly Muse Urania. The other love, that of Polyhymnia, is common and vulgar. It must be employed with great caution, so that one may reap its pleasure without sowing the seeds of licentiousness. [187e] In our art, it is a considerable challenge to properly manage the desires related to the culinary arts, to enjoy their pleasure without risking illness.

[188a] In music, medicine, and all other domains, both human and divine, we must, as far as possible, preserve both types of love, for both are present. Consider the composition of the seasons: when the elements I mentioned earlier—hot and cold, dry and moist—are influenced by the orderly kind of love and achieve a harmonious and temperate blend, they bring prosperity and health to humans, animals, and plants, doing no harm. [188b] But when the wanton love becomes dominant in the seasons, it brings destruction and injury. It is from such conditions that plagues and many other disparate

diseases afflict animals and plants. Frosts, hail, and crop diseases arise from the imbalance and disorder in the love relationships of such elements. The science that studies the movements of the stars and the seasons of the years is called astronomy.

Furthermore, all sacrifices and the realm over which divination presides—which foster the communion between gods and humans—[188c] are concerned solely with the preservation and healing of Love. For all impiety tends to arise when one fails to gratify or honor the orderly Love, instead favoring the other in all actions, whether towards parents, living or dead, or towards the gods. It is the task of divination to monitor and heal these matters of love, and thus divination is the creator of friendship between gods and humans, through its knowledge of human love affairs that tend towards piety and righteousness.

[188d] Thus, Love as a whole possesses a vast and mighty, or rather, an absolute power. But it is the Love concerned with good things, consummated with moderation and justice, both among us and among the gods, that holds the greatest power. It is this Love that provides us with all happiness, enabling us to associate with and befriend one another, and even with the gods, our superiors.

[188e] Perhaps I too, in praising Love, have omitted much, though not intentionally. If I have left anything out, it is your task, Aristophanes, to complete it. Or if you have in mind to eulogize the god in some other way, please do so, now that your hiccups have ceased."

[189a] Aristophanes, having recovered from his bout of hiccups, began to speak. "Indeed, the hiccups have ceased," he said, "though not before I applied the sneeze treatment. It's curious how the orderly functions of the body crave such noises and tickles as a sneeze. The moment I induced it, the hiccups vanished entirely."

Eryximachus interjected, "My dear Aristophanes, be mindful of what you're doing. You're on the verge of making jests before your speech, compelling me to be vigilant for any hint of humor in your words. Surely you could deliver your discourse in peace?"

Aristophanes chuckled and replied, "You're right, Eryximachus. Let me retract what I've said. [189b] But please, don't stand guard over me. I'm not concerned about saying something humorous in my upcoming speech—that would be a boon and befitting of my muse—but rather about saying something ridiculous."

"You think you can loose your arrow and escape, Aristophanes?" Eryximachus retorted. "No, pay attention and speak as though you'll be held accountable. Perhaps, if I see fit, I'll grant you leniency."

[189c] "Well, Eryximachus," Aristophanes began, "I intend to speak in a manner quite different from you and Pausanias. In my view, humanity has utterly failed to recognize the true power of Love. If they did, they would build the grandest temples and altars in his honor, offering the most lavish sacrifices. Yet none of this occurs, though it should above all else. For Love is the most philanthropic of gods, [189d] the guardian of humankind and the healer of ills which, once cured, would bring the greatest happiness to the human race.

I shall attempt to reveal to you his power, and you shall become teachers to others. But first, you must understand human nature and its afflictions. For our nature was not always as it is now, but quite different. [189e] Originally, there were three kinds of human beings, not just two as there are now—male and female. There was also a third, a combination of both, which has since vanished, though its name remains: androgynous. It was a distinct form, a union of male and female, but now the term survives only as an insult.

[190a] The shape of each human was completely round, with back and sides forming a circle. They had four hands, an equal number of legs, and two identical faces on a circular neck. Between the two faces, which looked in opposite directions, was a single head with four ears. They had two sets of genitals and everything else as you might imagine from this description.

They walked upright, in whichever of the two directions they pleased. When they wanted to run fast, they would cartwheel, spinning rapidly with their eight limbs, like acrobats.

[190b] The three types were as follows: the male was originally the offspring of the sun, the female of the earth, and the androgynous of the moon, which partakes of both sun and earth. They were spherical in shape and in their motion due to their similarity to their parents.

They were terrible in their strength and vigor, and had great ambitions. They made an attempt on the gods, and Homer's story about Ephialtes and Otus scaling heaven to attack the gods is really about these creatures.

[190c] Zeus and the other gods deliberated on what to do with them. They were in a quandary, for they couldn't annihilate the race with thunderbolts as they had the giants—that would destroy the honors and offerings they received from humans—but neither could they allow such insolence to continue.

After much consideration, Zeus declared, "I believe I have a solution that will allow humans to exist while ending their insolence by making them weaker. [190d] I shall cut each of them in two. This will make them weaker, but also more useful to us as they will be greater in number. They shall walk upright on two legs. If they continue to be insolent and refuse to keep the peace, I'll cut them in two again, and they'll have to hop on one leg."

With that, he began to cut the humans in two, like someone slicing fruit for preservation, or eggs with a hair. [190e] As he cut each one, he ordered Apollo to turn its face and half its neck towards the cut, so that the human would see its own division and behave more modestly. Apollo was also to heal the rest of the body.

[191a] Apollo turned their faces around and, gathering the skin from all sides into what we now call the belly, like a drawstring purse, he tied it firmly in the middle, forming what we know as the navel. He smoothed out most of the wrinkles and shaped the chest, using a tool similar to that which cobblers use to smooth wrinkles in leather on a last. He left a few wrinkles around the belly and navel as a reminder of their ancient state.

Now, when the body was split in two, each half yearned for its other half. They would throw their arms around each other, entwining in mutual embraces, longing to grow together again. [191b] They began to die from hunger and inactivity, because they didn't want to do anything apart from each other. Whenever one half died and the other was left, the remaining half sought another and embraced it, whether it happened to be the half of a whole woman (what we now call a woman) or of a man, and thus they kept dying.

Zeus, moved to pity, devised another plan. He moved their genitals to the front—previously they were on the outside, and they would generate and give birth not into each other but into the ground, like cicadas. [191c] He relocated their genitals and enabled them to generate in one another, the male in the female. His purpose was twofold: if a man should encounter a woman, they might generate and perpetuate the race; but if male should meet with male, they might at least obtain satisfaction from their intercourse, take a rest, turn to their labors, and get on with their lives.

From that distant time, then, love is inborn in human beings, [191d] reassembling our ancient nature, endeavoring to make one out of two and to heal human nature. Each of us, then, is but a token of a human being, sliced in half like a flatfish, always searching for our corresponding token. Those men who are halves of the original androgynous being are lovers of women, and many adulterers come from this group; similarly, women who are drawn to men and prone to adultery are also from this group. [191e] Women who are halves of an original female pay little attention to men, being more drawn to women, and the lesbians come from this group.

[192a] Those who are sections of the male pursue males. As boys, being chips off the masculine block, they love men and delight in lying with them and being entwined in men's embraces. These are the finest of boys and youths, being naturally the most manly. Some say they are shameless, but this is false. It is not shamelessness that motivates them, but rather courage, manliness, and a virile spirit, as they welcome what is like themselves. There is strong evidence for this: when they reach maturity, these alone prove to be men in matters of state.

As adults, they become lovers of boys. Marriage and fatherhood do not naturally attract them, [192b] though custom may compel them. They are content to live together unwed. Such a man invariably becomes a lover of boys and a lover of love, always drawn to his own kind. When he—or indeed any lover—meets that very person who is his other half, he is overwhelmed by friendship, kinship, and love in a way that is truly astounding. [192c] They do not wish to be apart, even for a moment.

These are the people who pass their whole lives together, yet cannot even say what they want from one another. No one would think it is merely sexual intercourse that makes them so happy to be together. Instead, it's clear that each soul desires something else it cannot express, divining what it wants and hinting at it obscurely. Suppose Hephaestus stood over them as they lay together, tools in hand, and asked: "What is it you two really want from each other?"

And if they were at a loss, he might ask again: "Is this your heart's desire: to be joined as one so completely that you are never separated, day or night? If that's what you crave, I can fuse you together, [192e] so that two become one. Then, as long as you live, you'll live a single life, and when you die, even in Hades you'll be one departed soul instead of two. Consider if this is what you long for, and if it will satisfy you."

We know that not a single one would refuse this offer or express any other wish. Each would think he'd discovered what he had always wanted: to be unified and melded with his beloved, becoming one instead of two.

The reason for this is that our original nature was whole, and the desire and pursuit of that wholeness is called love. [193a] We used to be complete, but now, because of our wrongdoing, we have been split apart by the god—just as the Arcadians were by the Spartans. We must behave reverently toward the gods, or we risk being split again, left to hop about like figures carved in profile on a stele, sliced down the middle of our noses, half a person.

This is why every person should encourage complete piety toward the gods, [193b] so that we may escape this fate and attain the other, with Love as our guide and commander. Let no one act against Love —and whoever opposes the gods does act against Love. If we become friends with the god and are reconciled with him, we will discover and meet our true loves, which few manage to do nowadays.

And let not Eryximachus take my words as a jest aimed at Pausanias and Agathon. Perhaps they are indeed of this type and are both male by nature. [193c] But I speak for all, men and women alike, saying that our race would achieve happiness if we could bring our love to perfection and each find our true love, returning to our original nature. If this is best, then in our present circumstances, the closest we can come to it is best—and that is to find a love whose nature suits us. For this, we would rightly praise the god Love, [193d] who both helps us now by leading us to what is our own, and gives us high hopes for the future. If we offer piety to the gods, Love promises to restore us to our ancient nature, healing us and making us blessed and happy.

This, Eryximachus, is my discourse on Love, quite different from yours. As I asked before, please don't make fun of it, so we can hear what each of the others has to say—or rather, what each of the two remaining speakers has to say, Agathon and Socrates.

[193e] "I'll obey you," said Eryximachus. "Indeed, I found your speech quite pleasing. If I didn't know Socrates and Agathon to be experts in matters of love, I'd be quite worried they'd have nothing left to say, given how much and how variously the subject has been discussed. As it is, I'm still confident."

[194a] Socrates then said, "You've competed well yourself, Eryximachus. But if you were in my position—or rather, the position I'll be in after Agathon speaks—you'd be very afraid indeed and in quite a predicament, as I am now."

"You're trying to cast a spell on me, Socrates," said Agathon, "to make me nervous by suggesting that the audience has great expectations for my speech."

"I'd be forgetful indeed, Agathon," said Socrates, [194b] "if I thought you could be unnerved by a few people here, when I've seen your composure before a huge audience when presenting your own work."

"What's this, Socrates?" said Agathon. "Surely you don't think me so drunk with the theater that I don't know how much more intimidating a few wise people are than a large crowd of fools?"

[194c] "It wouldn't be right of me," said Socrates, "to think anything crude about you. I'm well aware that if you met people you consid-

ered wise, you'd pay them more regard than the masses. But perhaps we're not those wise people—after all, we were there in the theater, part of the crowd. But if you met other wise people, you might feel ashamed before them, if you thought you might be doing something shameful. Or what do you say?"

"You're right," he said.

"And you wouldn't be ashamed before the masses if you thought you were doing something shameful?"

[194d] At this point, Phaedrus interrupted and said, "My dear Agathon, if you answer Socrates, he won't care in the least what happens to our discussion, as long as he has someone to talk with, especially if they're handsome. I enjoy listening to Socrates in conversation, but I must look after our praise of Love and receive a speech from each of you. So let each of you render his tribute to the god, and then you can talk."

[194e] "Well said, Phaedrus," Agathon replied. "Nothing prevents me from speaking now. I'll have many more chances to converse with Socrates."

Now, I wish to begin by stating how I ought to speak, and then proceed with my speech. It seems to me that all who have spoken before have not truly praised the god, but rather congratulated humans on the blessings the god has bestowed upon them. Yet none has spoken of the god's own nature [195a] that gave rise to these gifts. There is but one proper method for praising anything: to explain through reason what qualities the subject possesses and what effects it produces. So it is right that we should praise Love first for what he is, and then for his gifts.

I declare that among all the blessed gods, Love—if I may say so without incurring divine wrath—is the most blessed, being the most beautiful and the best. His beauty manifests thus: first, Phaedrus, he is the youngest of the gods. He offers great proof of this claim himself, fleeing old age with winged haste, [195b] for old age clearly moves too swiftly for us. Love, by his very nature, detests age and keeps far from it. Instead, he forever dwells with the young, for as the old saying goes, "like attracts like." While I agree with Phaedrus on many points,

I cannot concur that Love is older than Cronus and Iapetus. [195c] On the contrary, I assert that he is the youngest of the gods, eternally youthful. Those ancient tales of the gods that Hesiod and Parmenides relate—if they speak true—happened by Necessity, not by Love. For there would have been no castrations, bindings, and other violent acts among the gods had Love been present. Instead, friendship and peace would have reigned, as they do now under Love's divine rule.

Thus, he is young, and more than young, he is delicate. [195d] A poet of Homer's caliber is needed to fully illustrate a god's delicacy. Homer speaks of Ate[3] as both a goddess and delicate—at least her feet—saying:

> *Her feet are soft, for on the ground*
> *She walks not, but treads on the heads of men.*

This, I think, beautifully demonstrates her delicacy, that she treads not on the hard but on the soft. We shall use the same proof for Love's delicacy. [195e] He walks not on the earth, nor on skulls, which are not particularly soft, but in the softest of all things he both walks and dwells. For he makes his home in the characters and souls of gods and men, and not in every soul indiscriminately, but when he encounters a soul of harsh character, he departs, and where he finds a gentle one, there he settles.

Always in contact, then, with the softest of the soft, in feet and in all ways, he must be most delicate. [196a] He is, therefore, youngest and most delicate, and in addition to this, he is fluid in form. For if he were rigid, he could not enfold himself around everything, nor enter and leave every soul unnoticed at first, if he were hard. A great proof of his proportionate and fluid nature is his graceful shape, which by universal agreement Love possesses in a remarkable degree. For between unseemliness and Love there is eternal combat. The beauty of his complexion is shown by his living among flowers, [196b] for Love never settles in anything—be it body or soul or aught else—that is flowerless or faded, but where there is a spot flowery and fragrant, there he settles and stays.

Concerning the beauty of the god, this much may suffice, though much remains unsaid. Of Love's virtue, we must next speak. The greatest point is that Love neither wrongs nor is wronged, either by god or man. For he suffers not by force, if he suffers at all —for force touches not Love—nor does he act by force, [196c] for every one in all things serves Love willingly. And what one agrees to with another willingly is just, as "the royal laws of the city[4]" declare.

But besides justice, Love partakes of the greatest temperance. For temperance is admittedly mastery over pleasures and desires, and no pleasure is stronger than Love. If they are weaker, they would be mastered by Love, and he would master them. And mastering pleasures and desires, Love must be exceptionally temperate.

In valor, [196d] "not even Ares can stand against" Love. For Ares does not possess Love, but Love possesses Ares—that is, Aphrodite's love, as the story goes. And he who possesses is stronger than the possessed. Thus, he who masters the most valiant of the rest must be the most valiant of all.

Of the god's justice, temperance, and valor, we have spoken. Of his wisdom, it remains to speak, and we must try, as far as possible, not to fall short. First, that I too may honor our craft as Eryximachus did his, [196e] the god is so wise a poet that he can make others into poets. At any rate, everyone becomes a poet, "even if before he had no music in him," whom Love touches. This we may take as evidence that Love is a good poet, in sum, in every kind of musical creation. For what one does not have or does not know, one can neither give to another nor teach another.

[197a] Who could deny that the creation of all living things is the wisdom of Love, through which all creatures come into being and flourish? But consider the realm of arts and crafts: do we not know that when this god is the teacher, the pupil becomes renowned and illustrious, while those untouched by Love remain in obscurity? Apollo discovered the arts of archery, medicine, and prophecy under the guidance of desire and love. [197b] Thus, even he may be counted among Love's disciples, as are the Muses in music, Hephaestus in

metalwork, Athena in weaving, and "Zeus in governing gods and mortals[5]".

Indeed, it was only when Love was born among them that the affairs of the gods were set in order—clearly through the love of beauty, for Love has no part in ugliness. Before this, as I mentioned at the outset, many terrible things happened among the gods, as the stories tell, due to the reign of Necessity. But once this god came into being, all good things arose for gods and mortals alike through the love of beauty.

[197c] Thus, Phaedrus, it seems to me that Love is himself first the most beautiful and the best, and then he is the cause of such qualities in others. An urge comes over me to speak in verse, declaring that it is he who brings:

> *Peace to men, calm to the sea,*
> *Stillness to the winds, and restful sleep in sorrow.*

[197d] Love empties us of estrangement and fills us with kinship. He initiates gatherings like this, where we come together in festivals, dances, and sacrifices. He offers gentleness and banishes savagery. He is generous with goodwill and miserly with ill will. He is gracious, kind, and admired by the wise and beloved by the gods. He is envied by those who lack him and treasured by those who have him. He fathers luxury, tenderness, opulence, grace, yearning, and desire. He cares for the good and disregards the bad. In anxiety, in fear, in longing, in [197e] expression he is our best guide, ally, comrade, and savior. He is the ornament of all gods and men, the most beautiful and best leader, whom every man should follow, singing beautifully in his honor and joining in the song that Love sings, charming the mind of every god and man.

Let this speech of mine, Phaedrus, be dedicated to the god—part playful, part moderately serious, to the best of my ability.

[198a] When Agathon finished speaking, Aristodemus said that all present burst into applause, declaring that the young man had spoken in a manner worthy of himself and of the god. Then Socrates,

looking at Eryximachus, said, "Well, son of Acumenus, do you think my fear from earlier was unfounded? Didn't I prophesy that Agathon would give an amazing speech and that I would be at a loss?"

"You were certainly prophetic about one thing," Eryximachus replied, "that Agathon would speak well. But I don't think you'll be at a loss."

[198b] "My dear man," said Socrates, "how could I not be at a loss —I or anyone else—when faced with speaking after such a beautiful and varied discourse? While it was all admirable, who could fail to be struck by the beauty of the words and phrases at the end? When I reflect that I won't be able to say anything nearly as fine, I'd almost run away in shame if I had anywhere to go. His speech reminded me of Gorgias, so much so that I actually experienced what Homer describes: [198c] I feared that Agathon would end by sending the Gorgon-like head of the terrible speaker Gorgias against my speech, turning me to stone with speechlessness. Then I realized how ridiculous I'd been when I agreed to join you in praising Love and claimed to be knowledgeable in matters of love, when in fact I knew nothing about how to properly praise anything.

[198d] In my foolishness, I thought one should tell the truth about the subject of praise, selecting the most beautiful truths and arranging them most suitably. I was quite proud, thinking I would speak well, knowing as I did the truth about giving praise. But now it appears that this is not the proper method of praise at all. Rather, the right way is to attribute to the subject the greatest and most beautiful qualities possible, whether true or not. If they are false, it doesn't matter. For it seems we were each told to give a speech that appeared to praise Love, not to actually praise him.

[198e] This is why, I suppose, you resort to every kind of speech and attribute everything to Love, describing him and his effects in such a way that he appears most beautiful and best—to those who don't know better, of course, not to those who know the truth. And such praise is indeed fine and impressive. But I didn't know this method of praise, [199a] and in my ignorance I agreed to take part in the praising. 'The tongue promised[6],' but the mind did not. So,

farewell to that approach. I won't praise in that manner—I couldn't if I tried. But I am willing to tell the truth in my own way, if you wish, speaking according to my own method, not competing with your speeches, lest I become a laughingstock. So, Phaedrus, [199b] decide if you still want to hear the truth about Love spoken with whatever words and arrangement come to me naturally."

Phaedrus and the others, Aristodemus said, urged him to speak in whatever way he thought best.

"Well then, Phaedrus," Socrates continued, "allow me to question Agathon on a few points, so that, having his agreement, I may speak from that basis."

"I allow it," said Phaedrus, "so ask your questions."

[199c] Socrates then began somewhat as follows:

"Indeed, my dear Agathon, you seemed to me to begin your speech well when you said that one should first show what kind of being Love is, and only then discuss his works. I very much like this beginning. Come then, since you've spoken so beautifully and grandly about Love's nature, tell me this: Is Love the sort of thing to be love of something, or of nothing? I'm not asking if it's love of a mother or father—that would be a ridiculous question, whether Love is love of mother or father—but it's as if I were asking about this very thing, 'father': Is a father the father of something, or not? [199d] You would surely tell me, if you wished to answer correctly, that a father is the father of a son or daughter. Isn't that so?"

"Certainly," said Agathon.

"And the same goes for 'mother'?" He agreed to this as well.

"Then," Socrates continued, "answer a bit more, so you may better understand what I'm getting at. If I asked, 'What about a brother? Is he, by the very nature of what he is, a brother to someone or not?' you would say he is."

"He is a brother to a brother or sister," Agathon replied.

[199e] "Now try to tell me about Love," said Socrates. "Is Love love of nothing or of something?"

"Certainly, it is of something," Agathon answered.

[200a] "Well then," Socrates said, "keep that in mind and tell me this: Does Love desire the object of its love, or not?"

"Most certainly," came the reply.

"Now, when Love desires and loves something, does it already possess what it desires and loves, or not?"

"Probably not," was the answer.

"Consider carefully," Socrates pressed on, "whether it's merely probable or actually necessary that desire is for something one lacks. Can one desire what one already has? [200b] To me, it seems absolutely necessary, Agathon. What do you think?"

"I agree," Agathon replied.

"Excellent. Now, would someone who is already tall wish to be tall? Or someone who is strong wish to be strong?"

"That's impossible, given what we've agreed upon."

"Indeed, for one who already possesses these qualities wouldn't lack them."

"True."

Socrates continued, "If a strong person wished to be strong, a fast person to be fast, or a healthy person to be healthy—someone might think that people who are and have these qualities still desire what they possess. [200c] To avoid such confusion, let me clarify: these people, Agathon, necessarily have these qualities in the present, whether they want to or not. How could anyone desire what they already have? But when someone says, 'I am healthy and want to be healthy,' or 'I am wealthy and want to be wealthy,' and expresses desire for what they already possess, we might say to them, [200d] 'You, who have wealth, health, and strength, wish to possess these things in the future as well. In the present, whether you wish it or not, you have them. So consider whether, when you say you desire what you presently have, you mean anything other than that you wish for your present possessions to continue into the future.' Would they agree to this?"

Agathon nodded in agreement.

Socrates pressed on, "Isn't this, then, to love something that isn't yet at hand, namely, the preservation and continuation of one's present state into the future?"

[200e] "Certainly," Agathon replied.

"So this person, and indeed anyone who desires, desires what is not at hand and not present, what one does not have, what one is not, and that of which one is in need. Such are the objects of desire and love, are they not?"

"Indeed," came the response.

"Come now," Socrates said, "let's review what we've established. First, Love is always love of something, and second, it's love of what one lacks, correct?"

[201a] "Yes," Agathon agreed.

"Now, recall what you said in your speech about the nature of Love. Or shall I remind you? I believe you said something like this: the affairs of the gods were arranged through love of beauty, for there is no love of ugliness. Wasn't that more or less what you said?"

"It was," Agathon confirmed.

"And that's quite reasonable, my friend," Socrates replied. "But if this is so, wouldn't Love be love of beauty and not of ugliness?"

Agathon agreed.

[201b] "And haven't we just agreed that Love desires what it lacks and doesn't have?"

"Yes, we have," Agathon said.

"Then Love lacks and does not possess beauty."

"Necessarily so," Agathon conceded.

"Well then, do you still say that Love is beautiful, if these things are so?"

Agathon replied, "It seems, Socrates, that I didn't know what I was talking about in my speech."

[201c] "Yet you spoke beautifully, Agathon," Socrates said. "But tell me one more small thing: don't you think that good things are also beautiful?"

"I do."

"Then if Love lacks beautiful things, and good things are beautiful, Love must also lack good things."

"Socrates," Agathon said, "I can't argue with you. Let it be as you say."

"No, my dear Agathon," Socrates replied, "it's the truth you can't argue with, for arguing with Socrates is not at all difficult."

[201d] "But I'll leave you be now. Instead, I'll try to recount for you a discourse about Love that I once heard from a woman of Mantinea, Diotima. She was wise in these and many other matters. In fact, she once helped the Athenians delay a plague for ten years by advising them on sacrifices, and she's the one who taught me the art of love. I'll try to go through her arguments based on what Agathon and I have agreed upon, [201e] as best I can on my own.

"First, Agathon, as you explained, we must discuss who Love is and what he's like, and then his works. I think the easiest way to do this is to follow the method of questioning that the stranger used with me. For I was saying things to her very much like what Agathon was just saying to me: that Love was a great god and that he was of beautiful things. And she refuted me with the very arguments I've used against Agathon, showing that, according to my own account, Love was neither beautiful nor good.

'What do you mean, Diotima?' I asked. 'Is Love ugly and bad then?'

'Hush,' she replied. 'Do you think that if something isn't beautiful, it must necessarily be ugly?'"

[202a] "Absolutely," I replied.

"And if something isn't wise, is it therefore ignorant? Or haven't you noticed that there's a middle ground between wisdom and ignorance?"

"What's that?" I asked.

"To have the right opinion without being able to give a reason for it. Surely you realize," she continued, "that this is neither knowledge —for how can an unreasoned thing be knowledge?—nor ignorance —for how can something that hits upon truth be ignorance? Correct opinion, then, is just such a thing, lying between understanding and ignorance."

"You speak the truth," I acknowledged.

[202b] "Don't force the issue, then. Don't insist that what isn't beautiful must be ugly, or what isn't good must be bad. It's the same with Love. Just because you've admitted he's neither good nor beautiful doesn't mean you should think he must be ugly and bad. He's something in between," she said.

"And yet," I protested, "everyone agrees that Love is a great god."

"Everyone who doesn't know, you mean," she retorted. "Or do you include those who do know?"

"I mean absolutely everyone."

She laughed and said, "How could those who don't even consider him a god at all agree that he's a great god, Socrates?"

[202c] "Who are these people?" I asked.

"You're one," she replied, "and I'm another."

"What do you mean?" I exclaimed.

"It's simple," she said. "Tell me, wouldn't you say that all gods are beautiful and happy? Or would you dare to say that any god is not beautiful and happy?"

"By Zeus, I would not," I said.

"And by 'happy,' don't you mean those who possess good and beautiful things?"

"Certainly."

[202d] "Yet you've agreed that Love, because of his lack of good and beautiful things, desires these very things that he lacks."

"I have indeed."

"So how could he be a god if he has no share in beautiful and good things?"

"It seems he couldn't be," I conceded.

"You see then," she said, "that you also don't consider Love to be a god?"

"What then," I asked, "is Love? A mortal?"

"Far from it."

"What then?"

"As in the previous cases," she explained, "he's between mortal and immortal."

"What do you mean, Diotima?"

"He's a great spirit, Socrates. Everything spiritual, you see, [202e] is between god and mortal."

"What power does it have?" I inquired.

"It interprets and transports human things to the gods and divine things to humans. On the one hand, it conveys prayers and sacrifices from below, and on the other, commands and rewards for sacrifices from above. Being in the middle of both, it fills the gap, so that the whole is bound together with itself."

[203a] "Through this spiritual realm, all the arts of divination flow —the craft of priests in sacrifice and ritual, in enchantments, prophecy, and sorcery. God doesn't mingle directly with humans; it's through the spiritual that all converse and dialogue between gods and humans takes place, whether in waking life or in sleep. One who is wise in these spiritual things is a spiritual person, while one who is wise in anything else—be it a craft or manual labor—is merely a mechanic. These spirits are many and varied, and one of them is Love."

"And who," I asked, "are his parents?"

[203b] "That's quite a tale," she said, "but I'll tell you anyway. On the day Aphrodite was born, the gods held a feast. Among them was Resource, the son of Cunning. When they had dined, Poverty came begging, as one might expect at a festival, and lingered by the gates. Now Resource, drunk on nectar (for wine did not yet exist), wandered into Zeus's garden and fell into a heavy sleep. Poverty, scheming in her neediness to have a child by Resource, lay down beside him and conceived Love. [203c] This is why Love became the follower and servant of Aphrodite, because he was conceived on the day of her birth. Moreover, he is by nature a lover of beauty, and Aphrodite is beautiful.

"Being the son of Resource and Poverty, Love's situation is as follows: First, he is always poor, and far from being delicate and beautiful as most suppose, he is tough, unkempt, [203d] shoeless, and homeless. He sleeps on the ground without bedding, lying in doorways and on roadsides in the open air. He takes after his mother, always living in need. But on his father's side, he schemes to get beautiful and good things. He is brave, impetuous, and intense; a skillful hunter, always weaving some stratagem; desirous of wisdom and resourceful in getting it; a lifelong lover of wisdom; a clever magician, sorcerer, and sophist. [203e] He is by nature neither immortal nor mortal. Sometimes on the same day he flourishes and lives when he has resources; other times he dies, but then comes back to life because of his father's nature. What he gains always slips away, so Love is neither resourceless nor rich. He stands, too, between wisdom and ignorance."

[204a] The matter stands thus: No god pursues philosophy or yearns to become wise—for a god is already wise. Nor does any other wise being philosophize. Conversely, the ignorant neither philosophize nor desire to become wise. This is the very curse of ignorance: to be content in one's own inadequacy, believing oneself sufficient when one is neither noble, good, nor intelligent. One who doesn't perceive a lack will never desire what they don't think they need.

"Then who," I asked, "are the philosophers, Diotima, if neither the wise nor the ignorant pursue wisdom?"

[204b] "Even a child could see," she replied, "that it must be those who fall between these extremes. Love would be among them. For wisdom is among the most beautiful things, and Love is the desire for beauty. It follows, then, that Love must be a philosopher, existing in the space between wisdom and ignorance. This nature comes from Love's parentage: born of a father who is wise and resourceful, and a mother who is neither wise nor resourceful. Such, my dear Socrates, is the nature of this spirit.

[204c] As for your notion of Love, it's no wonder you were mistaken. You thought, it seems to me, judging from what you said, that Love was the beloved rather than the lover. That's why Love appeared to you as wholly beautiful. For the truly lovable is indeed beautiful, delicate, perfect, and blessed. But the lover has a different form, such as I have described."

To this, I responded, "Very well, stranger, you speak beautifully. But if Love is of this nature, what use is he to humans?"

[204d] "That, Socrates," she said, "is what I shall try to teach you

next. Love is indeed as I have described, and he is of beautiful things, as you say. But if someone were to ask us, 'In what way, Socrates and Diotima, is Love of beautiful things?' Or more clearly: What does the lover of beautiful things desire?"

I answered, "That they become his own."

"But," she said, "this answer invites a further question: What will be the result when he obtains beautiful things?"

I admitted I couldn't readily answer that question.

[204e] "Well," she said, "suppose we substitute 'good' for 'beautiful' and ask: 'Socrates, what does the lover of good things desire?'"

"That they become his own," I replied.

"And what will be the result when he obtains good things?"

"This I can answer more easily," I said. "He will be happy."

[205a] "Yes," she said, "for it's through the possession of good things that the happy are made happy. And there's no need to ask further, 'Why does one want to be happy?' The answer seems to be complete."

"You speak the truth," I said.

"Now, do you think this desire and love are common to all humans? Do all people always want good things for themselves? Or what do you say?"

"Just that," I replied. "It's common to all."

"Then why, Socrates," she asked, "do we not say that everyone is in love, [205b] if indeed everyone always loves the same things? Instead, we say some people are in love, while others are not."

"I wonder about that myself," I said.

"Don't wonder," she said. "We've simply taken one form of love and applied the name of the whole to it, while using other names for the other forms."

"Like what?" I asked.

"Like this: You know that 'creation' is a broad term. Whenever something comes into existence that wasn't there before, the cause of this is always creation. [205c] So the productions of all arts are creations, and their craftsmen are all creators."

"True," I said.

"Yet," she continued, "you know they aren't called creators but have other names. From the whole realm of creation, one part is set apart—that which concerns music and meter—and is called by the name of the whole. Only this is called poetry, and those who possess this part of creation are called poets."

"That's true," I said.

[205d] "The same goes for love. Broadly speaking, all desire for good things and for happiness is 'the great and beguiling love' in everyone. But those who pursue this in various ways—through making money, or through the love of sports, or through philosophy —are not said to be in love, nor called lovers. It's only those who are devoted to one particular kind of love who are given the name of the whole—love, loving, and lovers."

"I think you may be right," I said.

"Now, there's a theory," she continued, "that lovers are those who seek their other half. [205e] But my view is that love is neither for the half nor for the whole, unless, my friend, that half or whole happens to be good. For people are willing to have their own feet and hands cut off if they think these parts of themselves are bad. People don't cherish what belongs to them unless they identify the good with what is their own and the bad with what is alien. For what people love is simply and solely the good."

[206a] "People don't simply love what belongs to them," she continued, "unless we define 'one's own' as 'good' and 'not one's own' as 'bad.' The truth is, people love nothing but the good. Don't you agree?"

"By Zeus, I do," I replied.

"Then, can we simply say that people love the good?"

"Yes," I answered.

"But shouldn't we add that they also desire to possess the good?"

"We should."

"And not just to possess it," she pressed on, "but to possess it always?"

"We must add that too."

"Then, in summary," she concluded, "love is the desire to possess the good forever."

"You speak the absolute truth," I agreed.

[206b] "Now that we've established this as the constant nature of love," she continued, "in what manner do people pursue it, and through what action does their earnest striving deserve to be called love? What is this deed? Can you tell me?"

"If I could, Diotima," I replied, "I wouldn't be in such awe of your wisdom, nor would I be seeking your guidance on these very matters."

"Well then, I shall tell you," she said. "It is bringing forth in beauty, both in body and in soul."

"Your words require a seer's interpretation," I said. "I don't understand."

[206c] "I'll explain more clearly," she said. "All human beings, Socrates, are pregnant in both body and soul. When we reach a certain age, our nature yearns to bring forth. But it cannot bring forth in ugliness, only in beauty. The union of man and woman is a bringing forth. This act is divine, for in mortal creatures, this is the immortal part: conception and generation. But these cannot occur in discord, and ugliness is discordant with all that is divine, while beauty is in harmony.

[206d] Thus, Beauty presides over birth as Fate and Goddess of Travail. When the pregnant approaches the beautiful, it becomes gentle and joyous, and gives birth and begets; but when it approaches the ugly, it becomes gloomy and distressed, shrinks away, turns aside, and does not beget, but holds back the offspring, suffering in pain. Hence, the pregnant and already swelling being is drawn to beauty with a powerful yearning, for beauty releases it from the great pain of childbirth.

[206e] For love, Socrates," she said, "is not of the beautiful as you suppose."

"What then?" I asked.

"It is of begetting and bringing forth in beauty."

"Let it be so," I said.

[207a] "Indeed it is," she affirmed. "But why of begetting? Because begetting is the closest a mortal being can come to perpetuity and immortality. And from our earlier agreement, we must conclude that the desire for immortality accompanies the desire for good, since love wants to possess the good forever. It follows from this argument that love must also desire immortality."

All these things she taught me whenever she spoke about love. And once she asked, "What do you think, Socrates, is the cause of this love and desire? Haven't you noticed the terrible state of all animals, both land creatures and birds, when they desire to procreate? [207b] They all become sick with love, first to mate with each other, then to nurture their offspring. For their sake, even the weakest are ready to battle the strongest and die for them, to starve themselves to feed their young, and to do anything necessary. One might think that humans do this from reason, but what causes animals to be in such a state of love? Can you explain?"

Again, I said I didn't know. She then asked, "Do you expect to become an expert in love if you don't understand this?"

"But that's why I've come to you, Diotima, as I just said. I know I need teachers. So please, explain this and the other mysteries of love to me."

[207c] "Well then," she said, "if you believe that love is, by nature, what we've often agreed it to be, don't be surprised at this. For here, as in our earlier reasoning, mortal nature seeks, as far as it can, to be forever and immortal. It can achieve this only through procreation, by always leaving behind a new young one in place of the old. [207d] Even during the period in which each living creature is said to live and be the same - as a person is said to be the same from childhood till old age - yet, though called the same, it never contains the same things in itself, but is always being renewed and losing what it had before, whether it's hair, flesh, bones, blood, or the entire body.

[207e] And not just in the body, but in the soul too: a person's manners, habits, opinions, desires, pleasures, pains, and fears never remain the same, but some are coming to be and others are passing away."

[208a] "But even more astonishing than this," she continued, "is how our very knowledge is in constant flux. Not only do we gain and lose different areas of expertise, never remaining the same in our understanding, but each individual piece of knowledge undergoes this same process. What we call 'study' is actually the replenishment of fading knowledge. Forgetfulness is the exodus of knowledge, while study implants new memories to replace the departing ones, preserving our understanding and creating the illusion of constancy.

"This, Socrates, is how all mortal things persevere. Unlike the divine, which remains eternally unchanged, [208b] mortal nature achieves a kind of immortality by leaving behind something new in place of the old. Through this clever mechanism, the mortal partakes in immortality – be it the body or anything else. The immortal takes a different path entirely.

"So, do not marvel that every creature naturally cherishes its offspring. It is for the sake of immortality that this zeal and love attend all beings."

I was awestruck by her words and exclaimed, "Is this truly so, wisest Diotima?"

[208c] She replied with the assurance of a master sophist, "Know it well, Socrates. If you consider human ambition, you would be amazed at the irrationality of their behavior – that is, if you haven't already grasped what I've explained. Observe how fiercely they desire to become renowned, to secure undying fame for all time. For this, they are ready to brave any danger, even more so than for their children. They will spend their fortune, endure any hardship, and even sacrifice their lives.

[208d] "Do you think," she asked, "that Alcestis would have died for Admetus, or Achilles followed Patroclus in death, or your own Codrus sacrificed himself for his children's kingship, if they didn't believe they would leave behind an immortal memory of their virtue – the very memory we now hold of them? Far from it," she asserted. "I believe that all people act for the sake of immortal virtue and glorious renown. The nobler they are, the more they strive, for they are in love with immortality.

[208e] "Those whose fertility is of the body," she went on, "turn to women, expressing their love through procreation. They believe that through their offspring, they secure for themselves immortality, remembrance, and happiness in the time to come. [209a] But those who are pregnant in soul – and yes, there are those whose souls are even more fertile than their bodies – conceive what is fitting for a soul to bear and bring forth. And what is fitting? Wisdom and virtue in all their forms. Among these soul-bearers are all the poets and those craftsmen deemed to be innovative.

"The greatest and most beautiful part of wisdom," she declared, "is that which concerns the proper ordering of cities and households, which we call temperance and justice. When a man's soul is ripe with these seeds from youth, [209b] and upon reaching maturity, he desires to give birth, he too will seek out the beautiful in which to engender them. For he will never bring forth in ugliness.

"In his fertile state, he embraces beautiful bodies more than ugly ones, and if he encounters a beautiful, noble, and naturally gifted soul, he embraces the two in combination even more. To such a person, he readily speaks about virtue, about the nature and pursuits of a good man, [209c] and attempts to educate him.

"Through contact with the divine beauty and in constant communion with it, he brings forth and nourishes what he has long carried inside. Whether present or absent, he holds it in his memory, and together they nurture their common progeny. Such men share a much closer partnership and a more enduring friendship than those based on children, for the children they share are more beautiful and more immortal.

"Anyone would prefer to have such children rather than human offspring. [209d] Looking upon Homer, Hesiod, and other great poets, one envies the children they have left behind – children that bring them immortal fame and remembrance. Or consider the children Lycurgus left behind in Sparta, saviors not just of Lacedaemon but of Greece itself. Solon, too, is honored among you for begetting your laws, and many other men, both among Greeks and barbarians, have brought forth great works, [209e] giving birth to every kind of virtue.

Many shrines have been raised to honor such offspring, but never for merely human children."

[210a] "These are the lesser mysteries of love, Socrates, in which perhaps even you could be initiated. But as for the final revelation, the ultimate vision for which these are but preparatory – I don't know if you are capable of it. Nevertheless, I shall explain and spare no effort. Try to follow if you can.

"The one who would pursue this matter correctly must begin in youth to seek out beautiful forms. At first, if guided rightly, he should love one beautiful body and generate beautiful discourses there. Then he must realize that the beauty in any one body [210b] is akin to that in another, and if he is to pursue beauty of form, it would be great folly not to regard the beauty in all bodies as one and the same. Once he grasps this, he must become a lover of all beautiful bodies, relaxing his intense passion for one alone as something petty.

"After this, he must come to appreciate that the beauty of souls is more valuable than that of the body. Thus, if someone has a beautiful soul, even if the bloom of youth has faded, [210c] it should be enough to love, care for, and bring forth such discourses as may improve the young. This will lead him to observe the beauty in customs and laws, and to realize that it is all of one family. He will then regard the beauty of the body as insignificant.

"From customs, he must be led to the sciences so that he may see the beauty of knowledge. No longer like a slave, in love with the beauty of a single thing – be it a boy, a man, or a single custom – [210d] he will instead turn to the great sea of beauty and, gazing upon it, give birth to many beautiful and magnificent discourses and thoughts in boundless love of wisdom.

"Until, strengthened and grown in this, he catches sight of a certain single knowledge, which is the knowledge of beauty such as this: [210e] Pay attention now, Socrates, with all your might!"

"For one who has been guided thus far in matters of love, contemplating beautiful things in their proper order and correctly, will suddenly behold at the very end of his erotic quest a wonder of beauty in its nature. This, Socrates, is that very thing for which all the prior labors were undertaken. Firstly, it is eternal, neither coming into being nor perishing, neither waxing nor waning. [211a] Secondly, it is not beautiful in one respect and ugly in another, nor beautiful at one time and ugly at another, nor beautiful in relation to one thing and ugly in relation to another; nor is it beautiful here but ugly there, as if beautiful to some and ugly to others. Nor will this beauty appear to him in the guise of a face or hands or any other bodily part, nor as any kind of speech or knowledge. It does not exist in something other than itself, such as in an animal, or in earth, or in heaven, [211b] or in anything else. Rather, it exists eternally and absolutely by itself and with itself. All other beautiful things share in it in such a way that, while they come into being and pass away, it neither increases nor diminishes, nor is it affected in any way.

"When someone, ascending from these earthly things through the right kind of love, begins to discern that supreme beauty, he has almost reached the goal. For this is the right way to approach love, or to be led by another: beginning from beautiful things here, to mount ever upwards for the sake of that ultimate beauty. [211c] As if ascending a staircase, one goes from one to two, and from two to all beautiful bodies; then from beautiful bodies to beautiful pursuits; from pursuits to beautiful learnings; and from these learnings he arrives in the end at that one learning, which is none other than the learning of that beauty itself, so that at last he comes to know what beauty truly is.

[211d] "At this point in life, dear Socrates," said the woman from Mantinea, "if at any point, life is worth living: when a man contemplates beauty itself. If you ever see it, it will not seem to you to be like gold or raiment or those beautiful boys and youths, at whose sight you are now so struck that you and many others, seeing these loved ones and being ever with them, would be content neither to eat nor drink, if that were possible, but only to gaze upon them and be in their company.

"What then," she said, "should we suppose it would be like [211e] if someone were to see the beautiful itself, pure, clean, unmixed, and unalloyed with human flesh or colors or any other mortal nonsense, but if he could behold the divine beauty itself in its unique form? [212a] Do you think," she said, "that would be a poor life for a human being, gazing in that direction and contemplating that object with the proper faculty and being in union with it? Do you not realize," she said, "that in that life alone, when he looks at beauty in the only way that beauty can be seen, will he be enabled to bring forth not images of virtue (because he's not in touch with images), but true virtue (because he is in touch with the truth)? And having brought forth and nurtured true virtue, he will have the privilege of becoming dear to the gods and, if any human being can, of becoming immortal himself."

[212b] "This, Phaedrus and all of you," she said, "is what Diotima told me, and I am persuaded by it. And being so persuaded, I try to persuade others that in the acquisition of this good, human nature can find no better helper than Love. Therefore, I say that every man should honor Love, and I myself honor and especially cultivate the matters of love, and I exhort others to do so, and now and always I praise the power and valor of Love so far as I am able. Consider this speech, Phaedrus, [212c] if you wish, as a eulogy spoken in honor of Love, or call it whatever you like."

When Socrates had finished speaking, the others praised him, but Aristophanes was beginning to say something in response to a reference Socrates had made to his speech. Suddenly, there was a loud knocking at the courtyard door, seemingly from a band of revelers, and they could hear the voice of a flute-girl. Agathon said, "Servants, go and see who it is. [212d] If it's someone we know, invite them in; if not, say we're no longer drinking but resting."

Not long after, they heard the voice of Alcibiades in the courtyard. He was very drunk and shouting loudly, asking where Agathon was and demanding to be taken to him. He was brought in, supported by the flute-girl and some of his companions, and he stood at the door, [212e] wearing a thick garland of ivy and violets and with a mass of ribbons on his head. He said, "Greetings, gentlemen! Will you welcome a man who is utterly drunk as a fellow drinker, or should we just crown Agathon, which was our purpose in coming, and be off?

For I tell you," he said, "I wasn't able to come yesterday, but now I'm here with these ribbons on my head, so that from my own head I may crown the head of the wisest and most beautiful man—if I may so describe him."

[213a] "Are you going to mock me for being drunk?" Alcibiades slurred. "Go ahead and laugh if you want, but I know I'm speaking the truth. Now tell me, shall I join you on your terms or not? Will you drink with me?"

A chorus of voices erupted, urging him to come in and recline. Agathon called out to him specifically. Alcibiades stumbled forward, guided by his companions, fumbling with his garlands as if to crown someone. With the wreaths obstructing his view, he failed to notice Socrates and instead took a seat between Socrates and Agathon, as Socrates had shifted to make room for him. As Alcibiades settled in, he greeted Agathon warmly and began to crown him.

[213b] Agathon then instructed, "Servants, remove Alcibiades' sandals so he can recline as the third in our group."

"Certainly," Alcibiades replied. "But who's this third drinking companion of ours?" As he turned, he caught sight of Socrates and leapt up with a start. "Good heavens!" he exclaimed. "What's this? Socrates, is that you? Lying in ambush for me again, are you? Popping up out of nowhere as usual, just where I least expect to find you. Why are you here? And why have you chosen this particular spot? [213c] Surely you're not next to Aristophanes or anyone else who's amusing and wants to be. No, you've maneuvered your way next to the most handsome man in the room!"

Socrates turned to Agathon and pleaded, "I may need your protection. This man's passion for me is no trifling matter. Ever since I fell for him, I haven't been able to so much as glance at or converse with another attractive person without him flying into a jealous rage. [213d] He does the most outrageous things - hurling abuse and barely keeping his hands off me. So please, make sure he doesn't do anything rash now. Try to reconcile us, or if he attempts any violence, defend me. I'm truly terrified of his mad devotion."

"There can be no reconciliation between us," Alcibiades declared.

"But I'll deal with you later for this. For now, Agathon, pass me some of those ribbons. [213e] I must crown this remarkable head of Socrates, lest he complain that I garlanded you but neglected him - he who conquers all in debate, not just once like you did yesterday, but always." With that, Alcibiades took some ribbons, crowned Socrates, and reclined.

Once settled, he announced, "Gentlemen, you all appear sober to me. This is unacceptable - you must drink! That was our agreement, wasn't it? I'll appoint myself master of the revels until you're all properly drunk. Agathon, bring out a large cup, if you have one."

[214a] Just then, Alcibiades spotted an enormous cooler that held more than eight quarts. He had it filled, drained it himself first, and then ordered it refilled for Socrates, saying, "My clever ploy is wasted on Socrates, gentlemen. No matter how much you tell him to drink, he'll drink it and never get drunk."

As the servant poured for Socrates, Eryximachus inquired, "What shall we do, Alcibiades? Are we just going to drink without conversation or song? That's hardly better than a group of thirsty men gulping down water."

[214b] Alcibiades responded, "Ah, Eryximachus, finest son of the finest and most temperate father, greetings to you!"

"And to you," Eryximachus replied. "But what do you propose we do?"

"Whatever you command," said Alcibiades. "We must obey you, for 'a doctor is worth many other men[7].' So, order as you see fit."

"Listen then," Eryximachus began. "Before you arrived, we decided that each of us, from left to right, should give a speech in praise of Love, making it as eloquent as possible. [214c] The rest of us have already spoken. Since you haven't given a speech and you've had your drink, it's only fair that you should speak. Once you've finished, you can choose any topic for Socrates, who will then pass it on to his right, and so on."

"That sounds fine, Eryximachus," Alcibiades replied, "but it's hardly fair to pit a drunk man's words against sober speeches. Besides, my dear fellow, did you actually believe what Socrates just said? [214d] You should know that it's quite the opposite of what he claimed. If I praise anyone else in his presence, be it god or man, he won't keep his hands off me."

"Watch your words!" Socrates interjected.

"By Poseidon," Alcibiades retorted, "don't deny it. I won't praise anyone else with you here."

"Well then," suggested Eryximachus, "why don't you praise Socrates?"

[214e] "What's that?" Alcibiades exclaimed. "Do you think I should, Eryximachus? Shall I attack this man and take my revenge in front of you all?"

"Hey now," Socrates said, "what are you up to? Are you going to praise me sarcastically? Is that your plan?"

"I'll speak only the truth," Alcibiades assured him. "Will you allow that?"

"Of course," Socrates replied. "I'd welcome the truth."

"Then I'll begin at once," Alcibiades declared. "And here's how we'll do it..."

[215a] "If I say anything untrue, Socrates, feel free to interrupt and correct me. I have no intention of lying deliberately. However, given my state of mind, don't be surprised if my recollections are somewhat jumbled. It's no easy task to recount your peculiarities in a neat, orderly fashion.

"Gentlemen, I shall attempt to praise Socrates through the use of similes. He may think I'm aiming for comedy, but my imagery is meant to illustrate truth, not to mock. I say he bears the strongest resemblance to those Silenus figures [215b] sitting in the sculptors' shops. You know the ones - crafted holding pipes or flutes, which, when split open, reveal statues of gods within. And I also liken him to the satyr Marsyas.

"Now, Socrates, you can't deny your physical resemblance to these figures. But let me explain how you're similar in other ways. You're quite the insolent fellow, aren't you? If you won't admit it, I'll bring witnesses. And aren't you a flute player? Indeed, you're far more marvelous than Marsyas. [215c] He charmed people with instruments, using the power of his mouth, as do those who now play his melodies. For whether a skilled flute player or a amateur flutist performs the tunes of Olympus - which I attribute to Marsyas, his teacher - his music alone has the power to possess and reveal those who are in need of the gods and their mysteries, because it is divine.

"You differ from him only in that you achieve the same effect with mere words, without instruments. [215d] When we hear anyone else speak, even a very skilled orator, none of us really care. But when we hear you, or even your words from another's lips, be the speaker man, woman, or youth, we are thunderstruck and possessed.

"For my part, gentlemen, were I not afraid you'd think me completely drunk, I'd swear under oath to the feelings his words have stirred in me - feelings that persist even now. [215e] When I listen to him, my heart races far more than any Corybantic reveler's, and his words bring tears to my eyes. I've seen many others affected the same way. When I listened to Pericles and other great orators, I thought they spoke well, but I felt nothing like this. My soul wasn't in turmoil or angry at my slavish state. But this Marsyas here has often left me feeling that life isn't worth living if I remain as I am. [216a] Socrates, you can't deny that this is true.

"Even now, I'm well aware that if I were to listen to him, I couldn't resist but would experience the same feelings. He forces me to admit that while I neglect myself, I still meddle in Athens' affairs. So I stop my ears and flee from him, as if from the Sirens, to avoid growing old sitting by his side. He's the only person before whom I've felt something you might not expect of me - shame. Yes, he alone makes me feel ashamed.

[216b] "I'm well aware that I can't argue against doing what he tells me to do, but when I leave his presence, I succumb to the honors bestowed by the masses. So I desert him and flee, and when I see him, I'm ashamed of what I've agreed to. Often I wish he didn't exist, but if that were to happen, I know I'd be even more distressed. I simply don't know what to do about this man.

"Such is the effect of this satyr's flute-playing on me and many others. [216c] But listen to how he resembles those figures I compared him to, and what remarkable power he possesses. Be assured, none of you really know him. But I will reveal him, since I've begun. You see how Socrates is enamored with beautiful young men, always surrounding himself with them, and enchanted by them. Then again, he seems to know nothing and be ignorant of everything. Isn't this just like a Silenus? Very much so. [216d] This is just his outer casing, like those carved Silenus figures. But when he's opened up, can you imagine how full of moderation he is inside, my fellow drinkers?

"Let me tell you: he cares nothing whether a person is beautiful - he despises this to a degree you can't imagine - or whether they're rich or have any other honor admired by the masses. He considers all these possessions worthless, and us too - I assure you. He spends his whole life playing and pretending with people. [216e] But when he's serious and opens up, I don't know if anyone has seen the godlike figures inside. I have seen them once, and they seemed to me so divine, golden, beautiful, and amazing that I simply had to do whatever Socrates asked.

[217a] "Thinking he was serious about my youthful beauty, I considered it a stroke of luck and a wonderful opportunity. I thought that by gratifying Socrates, I could hear everything he knew. You see, I was quite proud of my looks. With this in mind, I sent my attendant away one time - before this, I'd never been alone with him - and was left alone with Socrates. I must tell you the whole truth; pay attention, and if I lie, Socrates, you must correct me.

"So, gentlemen, I was alone with him, [217b] and I expected him to talk to me the way a lover would to his beloved in private. I was delighted. But nothing of the sort happened. He conversed with me as usual and spent the day with me, then left. After this, I invited him to exercise with me, hoping to make progress there. We exercised and wrestled together often, with no one else present. What more can I say? I made no headway.

"When I realized this approach wasn't working, I decided I had to pursue the man more forcefully and not give up, since I'd already begun. [217c] So I invited him to dinner, plotting just like a lover with his beloved. He didn't accept quickly, but eventually he agreed. When he came the first time, he wanted to leave right after dinner. I was too embarrassed to stop him then. But another time, after we'd finished dining, I kept talking late into the night. When he wanted to leave, I made an excuse about the late hour and persuaded him to stay. [217d] He rested on the couch next to mine, the same one where he'd dined, and no one else was sleeping in the room but us.

"Up to this point in my story, I could tell it to anyone. But you wouldn't hear what follows if, firstly, as they say, 'In wine, there is truth,' whether with children or without; [217e] and secondly, it seems unjust to me to cover up a magnificent deed of Socrates when I've embarked on his praise."

[218a] The affliction of one bitten by a viper now seizes me as well. They say that those who have suffered such a fate are unwilling to speak of their experience, except to fellow victims—for only they can understand and forgive the desperate words and actions born of such agony. I too have been bitten, and by something far more painful than any viper. My heart—or soul, or whatever one should call it—has been struck and stung by the words of philosophy. These words, more savage than any serpent, sink their fangs into the young and gifted soul, compelling it to say and do anything.

And now, as I look upon the faces of Phaedrus, Agathon, Eryximachus, Pausanias, Aristodemus, and Aristophanes—[218b] not to mention Socrates himself, and all the rest—I see that you have all shared in this philosophical frenzy, this Bacchic revelry. Therefore, you shall all hear my tale, for you will surely forgive both my past actions and my present words. But as for the servants, and any other profane or uncouth person who may be present, let them bar their ears with mighty gates.

Gentlemen, when the lamp had been extinguished and the servants had withdrawn, [218c] I decided it was time to abandon all pretense with Socrates and speak freely what was on my mind. I nudged him and said, "Socrates, are you asleep?"

"Not at all," he replied.

"Do you know what I have resolved?" I asked.

"What might that be?" he inquired.

"I believe," I said, "that you alone are worthy to be my lover, and yet you seem hesitant to broach the subject with me. My feelings on the matter are thus: I would be utterly foolish not to give myself to you in this way—or in any other way you might desire, be it my possessions or my friends. [218d] Nothing is more important to me than becoming the best person I can be, and I believe no one can help me achieve this more effectively than you. I would be far more ashamed to deny such a man as yourself than to indulge the whims of the foolish masses."

Upon hearing this, Socrates responded with his characteristic irony, yet in a manner true to his nature: "My dear Alcibiades, you must indeed be quite extraordinary if what you say about me is true, and if there is within me some power by which you might be improved. [218e] You must perceive in me a beauty beyond compare, far surpassing your own physical charms.

If, indeed, you have caught a glimpse of this and seek to share in it, to exchange beauty for beauty, then you aim to get the better of me by no small margin. You seek to acquire true beauty in place of its mere appearance, to trade, as it were, [219a] 'gold for bronze[8].' But my good man, look more closely, lest you be deceived and I turn out to be worthless. The mind's eye begins to see clearly only when the physical eye starts to fade, and you are still far from that point.

I replied, "I have spoken nothing but my true thoughts. It is for you to consider what you believe best for both of us."

"Well said," he answered. [219b] "In the time to come, we shall deliberate and do what seems best for us both in this and all other matters."

Having heard and spoken these words, I felt as though I had loosed arrows that had wounded him. I rose, not allowing him to utter another word, and wrapped him in my cloak—for it was winter —and lay down beside him under his threadbare garment. I embraced this truly divine and wondrous man, and remained there the whole night. [219c] And in this too, Socrates, you cannot say that I speak falsely.

Yet despite all my efforts, he utterly prevailed over me, showing disdain for my youthful beauty, mocking it—and it was this very thing, gentlemen of the jury (for judges you are of Socrates' arrogance), that I thought I possessed. Know well, by the gods, that I arose after sleeping with Socrates no differently than if I had slept beside a father or an elder brother.

[219d] Imagine, then, my state of mind after this experience—feeling at once slighted and filled with admiration for his character, his self-control, and his courage. I had encountered a man of such wisdom and strength as I never thought I would meet. I could neither find reason to be angry with him and deprive myself of his company, nor could I devise a way to win him over. [219e] I knew well that he was far more impervious to money than Ajax was to iron, and the one lure by which I thought I might catch him had proven ineffective. I was at a loss, utterly enslaved by this man as no one had ever been by another.

All this had transpired between us when we later went on the expedition to Potidaea[9] together, where we shared the same mess.

Firstly, in enduring hardships, he surpassed not only me but everyone else. Whenever we were cut off from our supplies, as often happens in campaigns, and forced to go without food, the others were as nothing compared to him in resilience. [220a] Yet in times of plenty, he alone could truly enjoy himself, especially in drinking—though he never wished to do so, when compelled he could outdrink anyone. Most astonishing of all, no one has ever seen Socrates drunk.

As for his endurance of winter's cold—and the winters there were terribly harsh—his feats were remarkable. [220b] Once, during a particularly severe frost, when others either remained indoors or ventured out muffled in an amazing array of clothes, with their feet wrapped in felt and fleeces, Socrates went out wearing nothing but his usual cloak, and walked barefoot across the ice with greater ease than others in their boots. The soldiers looked at him with suspicion, thinking he was mocking them.

[220c] And then there was that time on campaign when he did something truly extraordinary, worthy of your hearing. Lost in thought one morning, he stood in the same spot pondering some

problem. When he couldn't resolve it, he didn't give up but remained standing there, searching for an answer. It was already midday, and people began to notice, telling each other in amazement that Socrates had been standing there thinking since dawn. As evening approached, some Ionians brought out their bedding after dinner (it was summer then) [220d] and slept in the cool air while keeping watch to see if he would stand there all night.

And stand he did, until dawn broke and the sun rose. Then he offered a prayer to the sun and went on his way. If you wish to hear of his conduct in battle—for credit must be given where it is due—when the fight occurred from which the commanders awarded me a prize for bravery, it was none other than Socrates who saved me. [220e] He refused to leave me behind when I was wounded, and he rescued both my arms and me. I urged the generals then, Socrates, to give you the prize for valor, and this you cannot deny or claim that I speak falsely. But when the generals, mindful of my social standing, wanted to give me the award, you were even more eager than they that I should have it rather than yourself.

[221a] "Gentlemen, you should have seen Socrates during the retreat from Delium. I happened to be there on horseback while he was on foot in heavy armor. As our troops scattered in disarray, he and Laches were falling back together. I came upon them and immediately urged them to keep their spirits up, promising not to abandon them.

It was there that I had an even better opportunity to observe Socrates than I did at Potidaea. Being on horseback, I was less consumed by fear myself. First, I noticed how far he surpassed Laches in presence of mind. [221b] Then, Aristophanes, I couldn't help but think of your words – he truly seemed to be 'strutting like a proud rooster, eyes darting side to side[10]', calmly surveying both friends and foes alike. It was clear to anyone, even from a distance, that this was a man who would put up a fierce fight if challenged. This is why both he and his companion retreated safely. In battle, men like him are rarely attacked; it's the fleeing soldiers that the enemy usually pursues.

[221c] One could praise Socrates for many other remarkable qualities. While some of these traits might be found in others, what makes him truly extraordinary – worthy of utmost admiration – is that he is unlike any other person, past or present. One might compare Achilles to Brasidas and others, or liken Pericles to Nestor and Antenor. There are other such comparisons one could make. [221d] But this man is so unique in his strangeness, both in his person and in his words, that you won't find anyone remotely like him, no matter how hard you search, neither among those living nor those long gone. The only apt comparison, if any, would be to liken him not to any human, but to the sileni and satyrs – both his person and his words.

Oh, and there's something I initially forgot to mention: his words are also most like those sileni that open up. If someone were to listen to Socrates' discussions, they might at first seem utterly ridiculous. [221e] His words are cloaked in terms and phrases like the hide of a brazen satyr. He talks of pack asses, blacksmiths, cobblers, and tanners, [222a] and seems to be always saying the same things in the same ways. As a result, any inexperienced or foolish person would laugh at his words.

But if one were to see these words opened up and step inside them, they would find that these discussions are the only ones that have true intelligence within. Furthermore, they are most divine, containing a multitude of images of virtue, and extending to the broadest possible range of subjects – indeed, to everything that should be examined by anyone who aspires to be a good and noble person.

[222b] This, gentlemen, is my praise of Socrates. I've also included my criticisms, telling you how he insulted me. And he hasn't done this just to me, but to Charmides, son of Glaucon, Euthydemus, son of Diocles, and countless others. He deceives them all, playing the role of a lover, when in fact he ends up being the beloved instead of the lover. I'm warning you too, Agathon, not to be deceived by this man. Learn from our experiences and be cautious, lest you learn the hard way, as the proverb goes, 'like a fool after the fact.'"

[222c] When Alcibiades finished speaking, laughter erupted at his

frankness, as he still seemed to be in love with Socrates. Socrates then said, "Alcibiades, I think you're sober after all. Otherwise, you would never have so cleverly concealed your real purpose with such an elaborate screen, casually placing it at the end of your speech as if everything you've said wasn't aimed at driving a wedge between Agathon and me. [222d] You think I should love only you and no one else, while Agathon should be loved only by you and by no one else. But we've seen through your satyr play, your silenus act. My dear Agathon, don't let him get away with it. Make sure no one comes between us."

Agathon replied, "Socrates, you may well be right. I suspect this is why he placed himself between us, to keep us apart. But it won't work. I'm coming over to lie down next to you."

[222e] "Excellent," said Socrates. "Come and lie down on my other side."

"Good heavens!" exclaimed Alcibiades. "How I suffer at this man's hands! He thinks he must have the advantage over me in everything. But if not anything else, you wonderful man, at least let Agathon lie between us."

"Impossible," said Socrates. "You've praised me, and now I must praise the person on my right. If Agathon lies on your side, surely he'll have to praise me again before I praise him. [223a] So let him be, my friend, and don't begrudge the young man my praise. I'm quite eager to deliver his encomium."

"Bravo!" cried Agathon. "Alcibiades, there's no way I can stay here. I'm moving no matter what, so Socrates can praise me."

"There it is," said Alcibiades, "just what always happens. When Socrates is around, it's impossible for anyone else to get close to a beautiful person. Look how easily and persuasively he's found a reason for Agathon to lie next to him."

[223b] As Agathon was getting up to move next to Socrates, suddenly a large group of revelers arrived at the door. Finding it open as someone was leaving, they came straight in and made themselves at home. The place was filled with noise, and all order vanished as everyone was forced to drink large quantities of wine. Aristodemus

said that Eryximachus, Phaedrus, and some others left and went home. He himself fell asleep, and slept for some time, as the nights were long then. He woke towards dawn, as the cocks were crowing, [223c] to find that some guests were asleep and others had left. Agathon, Aristophanes, and Socrates were still awake, drinking from a large cup which they were passing from left to right.

Socrates was conversing with them. Aristodemus couldn't remember most of what they said – he'd missed the beginning and was also a bit drowsy. But the main point, he said, was that Socrates was compelling them to agree [223d] that the same person should know how to compose both comedy and tragedy, and that the skilled tragic poet should also be a comic poet. They were being forced to agree to this, though not entirely following the argument, and were starting to nod off. Aristophanes fell asleep first, then Agathon as day was breaking.

Socrates, having lulled them to sleep, got up and left, with Aristodemus following him as usual. He went to the Lyceum, washed up, and spent the rest of the day just as he always did. Then, in the evening, he went home to rest.

COMMENTARY

Introduction to the Commentary on "The Feast of Eros"

THIS COMPREHENSIVE COMMENTARY OFFERS AN IN-DEPTH ANALYSIS OF Plato's Συμπόσιον (Symposium), newly translated as "The Feast of Eros." This seminal work, a cornerstone of Western philosophy, presents a series of speeches on the nature of love (Eros) delivered at a drinking party in ancient Athens. The dialogue's enduring significance lies in its profound exploration of love, beauty, and the human condition, as well as its masterful integration of philosophical discourse with dramatic narrative.

Following the structure of the original dialogue, this exegesis provides detailed insights into each section of the text, from the opening frame narrative (172a) to the final scene of revelry (223d). By adhering closely to the text's progression, the commentary allows readers to trace the development of ideas and themes as they unfold, mirroring the experience of the dialogue's original audience.

The commentary begins with an examination of the framing device employed by Plato, where Apollodorus recounts the events of the symposium to an unnamed companion. This narrative strategy is analyzed for its implications on the reliability of the account and its role in establishing the legendary status of the gathering. The characterization of Apollodorus as a devoted follower of Socrates is explored, offering insights into the impact of Socratic teaching and the potential for philosophical devotion to border on fanaticism.

As the commentary progresses through each speech, it offers a nuanced analysis of the speakers' arguments, rhetorical strategies, and underlying philosophical positions. The civic-minded view of love presented by Phaedrus is contrasted with Pausanias' more complex division between common and heavenly love. Eryximachus' extension of love's influence to medicine and natural phenomena is examined for its reflection of holistic Greek thought. Particular attention is paid to Aristophanes' mythical account of love's origin, noting its enduring impact on Western conceptions of romantic love and its surprisingly progressive view of sexual orientation for its time.

The commentary devotes significant space to Socrates' pivotal speech, which introduces the teachings of Diotima. This section is meticulously analyzed for its presentation of Plato's theory of Forms, the concept of love as a "daimon" or intermediary being, and the famous "ladder of love" leading to the contemplation of absolute Beauty. The philosophical implications of these ideas are thoroughly explored, connecting them to broader themes in Platonic thought and their influence on subsequent Western philosophy.

Throughout the commentary, careful attention is paid to Plato's literary artistry. The use of dramatic irony, vivid imagery, and strategic interruptions (such as Aristophanes' hiccups) is examined for its contribution to the dialogue's philosophical content. The interplay between serious philosophical discourse and moments of humor or human frailty is analyzed, revealing Plato's skill in creating a text that is both intellectually rigorous and deeply engaging.

The commentary also provides rich contextual information, elucidating the historical, cultural, and intellectual backdrop of "The Feast of Eros." Greek social customs, particularly those surrounding symposia, are explained to help modern readers appreciate the significance of the dialogue's setting. References to mythology, historical events, and contemporary figures are clarified, offering insight into the world in which Plato was writing and the concerns that animated his philosophical project.

Special consideration is given to the portrayal of Socrates throughout the dialogue. His characterization as both a philosophical genius and a paradigm of self-control is examined, with particular attention to how this depiction serves Plato's broader philosophical and pedagogical aims. The tension between Socrates' approach to love and conventional Athenian values is explored, highlighting the dialogue's role in challenging societal norms.

The commentary concludes with an analysis of Alcibiades' unexpected entrance and speech, examining how this dramatic turn serves to ground the preceding philosophical discussions in lived experience. The complex relationship between Alcibiades and Socrates is scrutinized for its illustration of the challenges and potential pitfalls of philosophical eros.

Throughout, this commentary seeks to illuminate the enduring relevance of "The Feast of Eros" to discussions of love, desire, and the pursuit of wisdom. By unpacking the complex ideas presented in the dialogue, tracing their development, and contextualizing them within broader philosophical frameworks, this analysis aims to enrich the reader's engagement with Plato's timeless masterpiece.

Whether approached by students of philosophy, scholars of classical literature, or curious general readers, this commentary serves as an invaluable guide through one of the most celebrated texts in the Western canon. It invites readers to partake in the intellectual feast that is "The Feast of Eros," revealing the depths of Plato's insights and the artistry with which he presents them, while fostering a deeper understanding of love, beauty, and the philosophical life.

From 172A to 174e

Plato opens his dialogue with a framing narrative that serves multiple purposes. Apollodorus, the primary narrator, recounts the story of the dinner party to an unnamed companion. This narrative structure creates distance from the events, emphasizing their legendary status while also allowing Plato to comment on the reliability of the account.

Apollodorus is characterized as a devoted follower of Socrates, bordering on fanaticism. His harsh self-criticism and disdain for non-philosophical pursuits reveal the transformative impact of Socratic teaching, while also hinting at the potential for extremism in philosophical devotion.

Socrates is immediately set apart from others. His unusual appearance - freshly bathed and wearing sandals - highlights the special nature of Agathon's gathering. Socrates' tendency to fall into deep thought, even while walking, illustrates his constant engagement with philosophical reflection.

The text introduces key themes that will be explored in the dialogue, particularly the nature of love and the relationship between beauty and wisdom. The playful discussion about uninvited guests foreshadows the unexpected turns the evening will take.

Plato's use of literary allusions, particularly to Homer, demonstrates the intellectual climate of the time and the way in which classical texts were reinterpreted and challenged. The misquotation of the proverb about "good men" going to feasts uninvited serves both as humor and as a subtle critique of traditional wisdom.

The dinner party setting provides insight into Athenian social customs among the educated elite. The celebration of Agathon's tragic victory places the dialogue in a specific historical and cultural context, linking philosophical discourse to artistic achievement.

Plato's skillful narrative technique builds anticipation for the speeches to come, while also establishing the complex relationships between the characters, particularly the reverence shown towards Socrates by his followers.

FROM 175A TO 175C

This passage introduces Socrates' characteristic eccentricity. His habit of becoming lost in thought, even to the point of standing motionless in a neighbor's doorway, is presented as a well-known quirk by Aristodemus. This behavior sets Socrates apart from the other guests and emphasizes his philosophical nature, always ready to contemplate deeply at a moment's notice.

The text also provides insight into the social customs of the feast. Agathon, as the host, displays his generosity by instructing the servants to serve freely, as if the guests were the hosts. This reversal of roles highlights the convivial atmosphere of these gatherings.

FROM 175C TO 175e

The exchange between Socrates and Agathon is rich with irony and philosophical undertones. Socrates' metaphor of wisdom flowing like water between cups is a playful jab at Agathon's recent theatrical success. By comparing his own wisdom to a dream and Agathon's to a brilliant light, Socrates employs his famous irony, subtly questioning the nature of wisdom and knowledge.

Agathon's retort about putting their wisdom to the test, with Dionysus as judge, cleverly ties into the feast's drinking context while also hinting at the competitive nature of philosophical discourse.

FROM 176A TO 176e

The group's discussion about drinking reveals the aftermath of the previous night's excesses and showcases the feast as a regular occurrence for these men. Eryximachus, speaking as a physician, advocates for moderation, demonstrating the Greeks' awareness of the harmful effects of excessive drinking.

The decision-making process illustrates the democratic nature of these gatherings, with each member voicing their opinion before reaching a consensus. The group's choice to focus on conversation rather than heavy drinking sets the stage for the philosophical discussions to follow in the dialogue.

Eryximachus' final proposal to dismiss the flute-girl and engage in conversation instead of entertainment marks a shift from typical feast activities to a more intellectually focused gathering, setting the tone for the remainder of Plato's work.

From 177a to 180a

Phaedrus begins the series of speeches on love by emphasizing its divine nature and antiquity. He draws on various mythological and literary sources to establish Love (Eros) as one of the oldest gods, citing Hesiod's Theogony and Parmenides. This appeal to ancient authority serves to elevate the status of Love in the pantheon of Greek deities.

Phaedrus then argues that Love is the source of the greatest blessings for humans, particularly in inspiring noble behavior. He introduces the concept of love as a motivator for virtue, shame as a deterrent from disgraceful acts, and honor as an incentive for noble deeds. This idea of love as a moral force is central to his argument and reflects Greek cultural values of the time.

The speaker presents a idealized vision of a city or army composed of lovers and beloveds, suggesting that such a force would be invincible due to their mutual desire to appear honorable in each other's eyes. This concept, while romanticized, reflects the Greek practice of paiderastia, an institutionalized relationship between an older man (erastes) and a younger male (eromenos), which was seen as a means of education and character development.

Phaedrus supports his argument with mythological examples. He cites Alcestis, who sacrificed her life for her husband, as an exemplar of love's power to inspire self-sacrifice. The contrast between Orpheus and Achilles further illustrates his point: Orpheus, who failed to die for his love, is punished, while Achilles, who chose to avenge his lover Patroclus even at the cost of his own life, is rewarded by the gods.

These mythological references serve a dual purpose: they provide evidence for Phaedrus' claims about love's power and they appeal to the cultural knowledge shared by his audience. The emphasis on self-sacrifice and courage in love reflects Greek ideals of heroism and honor.

Phaedrus' speech sets the tone for the feast, presenting love as a divine, ennobling force that inspires the greatest human virtues. His argument, while rooted in Greek cultural context, introduces themes of love's transformative power that continue to resonate in modern discussions of love and relationships.

FROM 180B to 182d

Pausanias begins his speech by critiquing the simplistic approach to praising love, arguing for a more nuanced understanding. He introduces a dichotomy between two types of love, associated with two different Aphrodites: Heavenly and Common (Aphrodite Urania and Aphrodite Pandemos). This distinction forms the core of his argument and reflects the Greek tendency to categorize and analyze complex concepts.

The speaker's description of Heavenly Love as exclusively male-oriented and focused on intellect rather than physical beauty reveals the cultural values of ancient Greek society, particularly its emphasis on homosocial relationships and the cultivation of wisdom. In contrast, Common Love is portrayed as indiscriminate and base, encompassing both heterosexual and homosexual desires.

Pausanias's discussion of pederasty - the relationship between an older man and a younger male - is presented as an ideal when governed by Heavenly Love. He argues that such relationships should begin only when the younger partner has developed intellectually, emphasizing the mentorship aspect over physical attraction. This reflects the complex attitudes towards age and sexuality in ancient Greek culture, which differ significantly from modern perspectives.

The political dimension of love is explored through the example of tyrannical governments fearing strong bonds between citizens. Pausanias cites the historical example of Harmodius and Aristogeiton, whose love-inspired partnership led to the overthrow of the

Peisistratid tyranny in Athens. This illustrates the Greek understanding of love as a potentially powerful political force.

Throughout his speech, Pausanias employs rhetorical techniques such as antithesis (contrasting Heavenly and Common Love) and appeals to cultural authority (referencing Homer and Aeschylus). His argument is structured to present Heavenly Love as superior, aligning with Athenian ideals of nobility and virtue.

The complexity of Athenian law regarding love, as described by Pausanias, reflects the sophisticated and often contradictory attitudes towards relationships in ancient Greek society. His critique of other cultures' laws on love serves to position Athens as more enlightened, despite the acknowledged difficulty in understanding its nuanced approach.

FROM 182E TO 184a

Pausanias presents a complex view of Athenian attitudes towards love between men. He highlights the paradoxical nature of societal norms, where lovers are granted extraordinary license for behavior that would be considered shameful in any other context. This passage reveals the cultural acceptance of same-sex relationships in ancient Athens, but also hints at the strict social codes governing such relationships.

The speaker distinguishes between two types of love: base and noble. Base love, associated with physical attraction, is characterized as fleeting and superficial. In contrast, noble love is presented as enduring and focused on the cultivation of virtue and wisdom. This dichotomy reflects Plato's philosophical interest in the nature of love and its potential for spiritual and intellectual elevation.

Pausanias's argument that there is no such thing as a "lover's oath" provides insight into the ancient Greek understanding of divine law and its intersection with human affairs. This concept would be unfamiliar to most modern readers and highlights the cultural gap between ancient and contemporary views on love and commitment.

. . .

FROM 184A TO 185E

The text outlines a system of courtship that emphasizes restraint and careful assessment. This "testing" of lovers serves to separate those driven by base desires from those seeking noble connections. The emphasis on time and character over wealth or political influence reveals the value placed on genuine emotional and intellectual bonds in Athenian society.

Pausanias introduces the idea of "willing servitude" in the pursuit of virtue as the only honorable path in love. This concept aligns with Plato's broader philosophical themes of self-improvement and the pursuit of wisdom. The ideal relationship described here is one of mutual growth and education, reflecting the Greek concept of paideia, or cultural education.

The commentary on deception in relationships provides a nuanced view of honor and shame in Athenian culture. Pausanias argues that being deceived while pursuing virtue is still honorable, while being deceived for material gain is shameful. This distinction underscores the paramount importance of intention and character in Greek ethical thought.

The passage concludes with a transition to Aristophanes' speech, interrupted by his hiccups. This humorous interlude serves to lighten the tone after the dense philosophical discussion and showcases Plato's skill in crafting a lively and engaging dialogue.

FROM 186A TO 186E

Eryximachus, a physician, expands on Pausanias' concept of dual love by applying it to the realm of medicine and the natural world. He argues that love's influence extends beyond human relationships to all aspects of existence. This expansion of love's scope reflects the Greek philosophical tendency to seek universal principles.

Eryximachus introduces the idea of balance and harmony in medicine, drawing parallels between health in the body and moral behavior in society. His description of the physician's role in managing different "loves" within the body echoes the Greek concept of balance between opposing forces, a fundamental principle in ancient medicine.

The mention of Asclepius, the god of medicine, serves to give divine authority to Eryximachus' medical theories, a common practice in ancient Greek discourse.

FROM 187A TO 187e

Eryximachus extends his medical analogy to other fields, including music. His reference to Heraclitus' philosophy of unity in opposition demonstrates the interconnectedness of Greek philosophical thought. The discussion of harmony in music as a reconciliation of opposites further reinforces the theme of balance.

The physician's analysis of music introduces the concept of education (paideia) as the correct application of harmony and rhythm. This reflects the Greek belief in the moral and educational power of music.

Eryximachus' distinction between heavenly and common love, associated with different muses, echoes Pausanias' earlier division but applies it to a broader context.

FROM 188A TO 188e

The speech concludes by applying the concept of dual love to natural phenomena and religious practices. Eryximachus argues that proper balance in love influences everything from weather patterns to the relationship between gods and humans. This expansive view reflects the holistic nature of ancient Greek thought, which often sought to explain all phenomena through unified principles.

The mention of divination and sacrifices highlights the interconnectedness of medicine, natural philosophy, and religious practice in ancient Greek culture.

Eryximachus' final praise of love as the source of all happiness and proper relationships between mortals and gods serves as a culmination of his argument, emphasizing love's central role in all aspects of existence.

FROM 189A TO 191E

Aristophanes' speech presents a mythical origin of love through a fantastical tale of ancient human nature. The comic playwright begins with a humorous anecdote about his hiccups, setting a lighter tone before delving into his more profound narrative.

The myth Aristophanes constructs is both whimsical and philosophically rich. He describes primordial humans as round beings with four arms, four legs, and two faces. This imagery serves as an allegory for human wholeness and completeness. The three types of beings - male, female, and androgynous - correspond to the sun, earth, and moon respectively, reflecting ancient Greek cosmological beliefs.

Aristophanes' story echoes other Greek myths of hubris and divine punishment. The reference to Ephialtes and Otus, giants who attempted to scale Mount Olympus, connects this new myth to established Greek mythology. Zeus's decision to split humans as punishment for their arrogance is reminiscent of other divine punishments in Greek myths.

The act of splitting humans serves as Aristophanes' explanation for the origin of love and sexual desire. The yearning for one's other half becomes a metaphor for love, presenting it as a force that drives humans to seek completion. This concept of love as a search for one's other half has had a lasting impact on Western conceptions of romantic love.

Aristophanes' explanation for different sexual orientations is noteworthy for its time. He presents homosexuality and heterosexuality as equally natural outcomes of this mythical division, reflecting a degree of acceptance in ancient Greek society that contrasts with many later Western attitudes.

The speech's structure moves from the comic (the hiccup incident) to the mythic and then to the philosophical, demonstrating

Aristophanes' skill in weaving humor and profound ideas. His vivid imagery and narrative style make complex philosophical concepts accessible and engaging.

This myth serves as a centerpiece in the dialogue, offering a unique perspective on love that contrasts with and complements the other speeches in the dialogue. Aristophanes' contribution adds depth and variety to the overall discussion of love's nature and origins.

FROM 192A TO 194E

Aristophanes presents a mythical origin of love, describing humans as originally whole beings split by the gods. This myth serves as an allegory for the human desire for completion through love. The speaker argues that homosexual love between men is the most noble, as it stems from the most courageous and manly natures. This view reflects ancient Greek attitudes towards pederasty, which modern readers should understand within its historical context.

The concept of soulmates emerges from this myth, with Aristophanes suggesting that true happiness comes from finding one's other half. This idea has had a lasting impact on Western conceptions of romantic love. The speaker employs vivid imagery, such as Hephaestus offering to fuse lovers together, to illustrate the intensity of this desire for union.

Aristophanes connects love to piety, arguing that proper reverence for the gods - especially Eros (Love) - is necessary for human fulfillment. This links the personal experience of love to broader societal and religious concerns.

The dialogue structure allows for commentary on the speeches themselves. Eryximachus' response and the exchange between Socrates and Agathon reveal the competitive nature of the feast and the characters' awareness of their audience. Agathon's nervousness about speaking after impressive speeches highlights the high stakes of this intellectual competition.

Socrates employs his characteristic irony in his exchange with

Agathon, subtly challenging the young poet's confidence while maintaining a façade of admiration. This foreshadows the philosophical confrontation to come between Socrates and Agathon.

Phaedrus, as toastmaster, intervenes to keep the dialogue on track, emphasizing the ritual nature of the speeches in honor of Eros. This moment of meta-commentary reminds the reader of the structured nature of the feast as a social and intellectual event.

FROM 195A TO 195b

Agathon begins his encomium by critiquing previous speakers for praising Love's effects rather than the god himself. This meta-commentary serves to position his speech as superior and more methodologically sound. He outlines a systematic approach to praise, emphasizing the need to describe Love's inherent qualities and their consequences.

Agathon's first claim about Love's youth contradicts traditional Greek mythology, which often portrayed older gods as more powerful. This bold assertion challenges conventional wisdom and sets the tone for an innovative interpretation of Love's nature.

The speaker employs vivid imagery of Love fleeing old age, personifying abstract concepts to make his argument more engaging. The old saying "like attracts like" is used to reinforce Love's association with youth, demonstrating Agathon's skillful use of proverbial wisdom to support his claims.

FROM 195B to 195e

Agathon directly contradicts Phaedrus' earlier speech, refuting the idea that Love is ancient. This disagreement highlights the dialectical nature of the dialogue, where speakers build upon and challenge each other's arguments.

The reference to Hesiod and Parmenides serves to contrast Love's reign with an earlier, more violent era of divine history. This juxtaposition emphasizes Love's pacifying influence and aligns with the feast's theme of exploring Love's nature and effects.

Agathon's comparison of Love to Homer's description of Ate demonstrates his rhetorical skill in drawing parallels between divine figures. The quoted verse about Ate's delicate feet is repurposed to illustrate Love's gentle nature, showcasing Agathon's creative use of poetic sources to support his argument.

The metaphor of Love dwelling in the "softest of all things" - the characters and souls of gods and men - adds a layer of abstraction to the discourse. This poetic description elevates Love from a mere physical entity to a spiritual force, aligning with the feast's philosophical exploration of Love's essence.

FROM 196A TO 196E

Agathon's portrayal of Love as fluid in form introduces a concept of adaptability and pervasiveness. This attribute allows Love to "enfold himself around everything," suggesting its universal influence and subtle power.

The speaker's argument for Love's virtue is structured around four cardinal virtues: justice, temperance, valor, and wisdom. This systematic approach reflects classical Greek philosophical discourse and lends authority to Agathon's praise.

The paradoxical claim that Love "neither wrongs nor is wronged" presents Love as existing beyond normal moral constraints, emphasizing its divine nature. Agathon's reference to "royal laws of the city" adds a civic dimension to his argument, connecting divine Love to human social order.

In discussing Love's valor, Agathon cleverly inverts the traditional hierarchy of gods by claiming Love's superiority over Ares. This assertion challenges conventional mythology and reinforces the central theme of Love's supreme power.

The final section on Love's wisdom introduces the idea of Love as a creative force, capable of inspiring poetry in others. This concept links Love to artistic inspiration, a theme that resonates throughout the dialogue and Greek thought more broadly.

Agathon's speech, while eloquent and structured, relies heavily on sophistry and clever wordplay. His arguments, though persuasive, often lack substantial philosophical depth, setting the stage for Socrates' subsequent critique and exposition on the nature of Love.

FROM 197A TO 197C

Agathon's speech reaches its climax with a grand portrayal of Love (Eros) as the source of all creation and artistry. He employs a rhetorical technique known as encomium, heaping praise upon Love by attributing to it the origin of various arts and crafts. Agathon associates Love with Apollo, the Muses, Hephaestus, and Athena, suggesting that even the gods are pupils of Love. This establishes Love as a primordial force, predating and surpassing the Olympian gods.

The speaker then makes a significant philosophical claim: Love brought order to the cosmos, replacing the reign of Necessity with beauty and goodness. This idea echoes Platonic concepts of form and chaos, suggesting that Love is a fundamental organizing principle of the universe.

FROM 197C TO 197E

Agathon's speech takes on a poetic quality, culminating in a verse praising Love's power to bring peace and calm. He then presents a series of antitheses and word-plays, typical of sophistic rhetoric, to emphasize Love's virtues. This section showcases Agathon's skill as an orator, but also hints at the superficiality of his argument, which will soon be challenged by Socrates.

FROM 198A to 198d

The narrative shifts as Apollodorus recounts Socrates' reaction to

Agathon's speech. Socrates' ironic praise of Agathon's oratory and his self-deprecating comments set the stage for his dialectical approach. He humorously refers to the Gorgon and the orator Gorgias, playing on the similarity of their names. This wordplay would have been appreciated by Plato's contemporary audience, familiar with both the myth and the famous sophist.

Socrates then reveals a key distinction in methods of praise: one that seeks to tell the truth about the subject, and another that aims to attribute the greatest possible qualities regardless of truth. This sets up the contrast between Agathon's flowery rhetoric and Socrates' upcoming philosophical inquiry.

FROM 198E TO 199e

Socrates begins his dialectical examination of Love by questioning Agathon. He establishes a pattern of asking about relational concepts (father, mother, brother) to lead up to his question about Love. This method, known as the Socratic elenchus, aims to expose contradictions in his interlocutor's beliefs.

The dialogue's tone shifts from the earlier grandiloquent speeches to a more focused, logical discussion. Socrates' questions lay the groundwork for his own conception of Love, which he will develop in the subsequent sections of the dialogue.

FROM 200A TO 201e

Socrates employs his characteristic method of elenchus, systematically questioning Agathon to expose contradictions in his beliefs about Love. The key argument developed is that desire, and by extension Love, is always for what one lacks. This leads to the paradoxical conclusion that Love, being desire for beauty and goodness, must itself lack these qualities.

Socrates builds his case through a series of logical steps:

1. Love desires the object of its love.

2. One cannot desire what one already possesses.
3. Therefore, Love must lack what it desires.
4. If Love desires beautiful and good things, it must lack beauty and goodness.

This reasoning cleverly undermines Agathon's earlier praise of Love as a beautiful and perfect god. Socrates' argument reveals a more complex view of Love as a force driven by lack or incompleteness.

The introduction of Diotima, a wise woman from Mantinea, serves multiple purposes. It allows Plato to present more advanced ideas about Love while maintaining Socrates' characteristic profession of ignorance. Diotima's foreignness and her role in averting a plague in Athens lend authority to the upcoming discourse, preparing the reader for a deeper exploration of Love's nature.

Socrates' recounting of his conversation with Diotima mirrors his current dialogue with Agathon, creating a layered narrative structure. This technique allows Plato to present a more nuanced and developed theory of Love while maintaining the dramatic context of the feast.

From 202a to 203e

In this passage, Plato presents a dialogue between Socrates and Diotima, a wise woman from Mantinea. Their conversation explores the nature of love and knowledge, challenging common assumptions about both.

Diotima introduces the concept of a middle ground between wisdom and ignorance, which she calls "correct opinion." This idea is crucial to Plato's epistemology, suggesting that one can hold true beliefs without fully understanding their foundations. This concept bridges the gap between complete knowledge and utter ignorance, a theme that recurs throughout the dialogue.

The discussion then shifts to the nature of Love (Eros). Diotima refutes the common belief that Love is a god, arguing instead that he is a spirit (daimon) – an intermediary between gods and mortals. This characterization of Love as a daimon is significant, as it places Love in a unique position to facilitate communication between the divine and human realms.

Diotima then narrates the myth of Love's birth, an allegorical tale that explains Love's dual nature. Born of Resource (Poros) and Poverty (Penia), Love inherits characteristics from both parents. This parentage accounts for Love's constant state of lack and desire, as well as his resourcefulness and persistence in pursuing his objects of desire. The myth serves as a metaphor for the human experience of love, which is often characterized by both abundance and scarcity, ingenuity and need.

The description of Love's nature is vivid and paradoxical. He is portrayed as both lacking and resourceful, poor yet scheming to obtain beauty and goodness. This complex characterization reflects the multifaceted nature of love as experienced by humans – a force that can be both enriching and impoverishing, elevating and debasing.

Plato's use of myth and allegory in this passage is masterful, blending philosophical concepts with vivid storytelling. The dialogue form allows for a dynamic exploration of ideas, with Socrates playing the role of the inquirer and Diotima the wise teacher. This literary approach makes complex philosophical concepts more accessible and engaging to the reader.

Throughout the passage, Plato challenges conventional wisdom about love, gods, and human nature. By presenting Love as a spirit rather than a god, and by emphasizing its intermediary nature, he invites readers to reconsider their understanding of love and its role in human life and spiritual development.

FROM 204A TO 204C

In this section, Diotima presents a nuanced view of philosophy and wisdom. She argues that gods and truly wise beings don't pursue philosophy because they're already wise. The ignorant don't seek wisdom either, unaware of their own limitations. Philosophers, then, occupy a middle ground between wisdom and ignorance.

Diotima then introduces a crucial concept: Love as a philosopher. This personification of Love (Eros in Greek) as a seeker of wisdom is a central idea in Plato's thought. Love's parentage—a wise, resourceful father and an unwise, resourceless mother—symbolizes its dual nature, straddling wisdom and ignorance.

Socrates' misconception about Love being the beloved rather than the lover is corrected, highlighting the active, seeking nature of Love.

FROM 204D TO 205a

Diotima guides Socrates through a logical progression, moving from the love of beautiful things to the love of good things. This shift is significant in Greek philosophy, where beauty and goodness are often closely linked. The ultimate goal of love, according to Diotima, is happiness through the possession of good things.

FROM 205B TO 205e

Diotima introduces an important distinction between the broad concept of love and its specific manifestations. She uses an analogy with "creation" and "poetry" to illustrate how a general term can be applied to a specific instance. This leads to the idea that while all humans desire good things and happiness, only certain pursuits are traditionally labeled as "love."

The passage concludes with a critique of the popular notion that lovers seek their "other half," a reference to Aristophanes' speech earlier in the dialogue. Diotima argues instead that love is fundamentally about seeking the good, even if it means sacrificing parts of oneself. This idea challenges conventional notions of love and self-interest, suggesting a more profound understanding of human desire and the nature of goodness.

. . .

FROM 206A TO 207E

Diotima, a wise woman from Mantinea, guides Socrates through a sophisticated analysis of love's nature. She begins by refining the concept of love, asserting that people love what is good and desire to possess it eternally. This sets the stage for her broader argument about love's connection to immortality.

Diotima introduces the pivotal concept of "bringing forth in beauty" (τόκος ἐν καλῷ), which she presents as the essence of love. This idea encompasses both physical procreation and the generation of ideas or virtues in the soul. The Greek word "τόκος" (tokos) means both "birth" and "interest on a loan," suggesting that love's productivity is both natural and beneficial.

The text draws a parallel between divine creation and human procreation, elevating the act of reproduction to a sacred status. Diotima personifies Beauty (Καλλονή) as presiding over birth, associating it with Fate (Μοῖρα) and Eileithyia, the Greek goddess of childbirth. This metaphysical framework presents beauty as a necessary condition for creation, whether physical or intellectual.

Diotima's argument culminates in the revelation that love is not of beauty itself, but of "begetting and bringing forth in beauty." This subtle distinction shifts the focus from passive appreciation to active creation, aligning with the Greek ideal of productive virtue.

The dialogue then transitions to a discussion of immortality through generation. Diotima argues that mortal beings strive for immortality through procreation, leaving behind new life as the old passes away. This concept extends beyond physical reproduction to include the perpetuation of ideas, customs, and knowledge.

Diotima's method of questioning Socrates exemplifies the Socratic method, ironically turned on its usual practitioner. Her series of leading questions gradually builds a complex philosophical argument, demonstrating the dialectical approach characteristic of Plato's works.

The passage concludes with a profound observation about the impermanence of individual identity. Diotima points out that even as we consider ourselves the same person throughout our lives, we are constantly changing both physically and mentally. This concept challenges notions of fixed identity and underscores the theme of perpetual renewal through love and creation.

From 208a to 208e

Diotima expounds on the nature of mortal existence and its pursuit of immortality. She introduces a fascinating concept of knowledge as something in constant flux, comparing the process of learning to a continuous replacement of fading memories with new ones. This idea challenges the notion of static knowledge and introduces a dynamic view of human understanding.

The text then shifts to a broader discussion of how mortal beings strive for immortality. Diotima argues that all mortal things, including the body and knowledge, persist through a process of constant renewal. This concept of renewal as a form of immortality is central to her argument and provides a foundation for understanding human behavior and ambition.

Diotima cites several mythological and historical figures to illustrate her point about the human desire for immortal fame. Alcestis, who died in place of her husband, and Achilles, who chose a short, glorious life over a long, unremarkable one, exemplify this pursuit of eternal renown. Codrus, a legendary Athenian king who sacrificed himself for his city, further reinforces this idea. These references would have been familiar to Plato's contemporary audience but might require explanation for modern readers.

From 209a to 209e

Diotima introduces a crucial distinction between physical and spiritual procreation. Those "pregnant in body" seek immortality through biological children, while those "pregnant in soul" create lasting works of art, literature, or law. This metaphor of mental pregnancy and birth is a recurring theme in Plato's works, notably in the "Theaetetus."

She elevates intellectual and creative pursuits, suggesting that the "children" of the mind - ideas, poems, laws - are superior to physical offspring in achieving immortality. Diotima cites Homer, Hesiod, Lycurgus, and Solon as examples of men who have achieved immortality through their intellectual legacies. This passage reflects the Greek reverence for poets and lawgivers, positioning them as exemplars of the highest form of love - the love of wisdom and virtue.

FROM 210A TO 210e

In this section, Diotima outlines a ladder of love, describing a philosophical ascent from the love of physical beauty to the contemplation of abstract Beauty itself. This concept is central to Platonic philosophy, representing the journey from the material world of appearances to the realm of Forms or Ideas.

The progression she describes - from loving one beautiful body, to all beautiful bodies, to beautiful souls, to beautiful laws and institutions, and finally to the Form of Beauty itself - is a key element of Platonic epistemology and metaphysics. It suggests that true understanding and wisdom come from moving beyond particular instances to grasp universal principles.

Diotima's insistence that Socrates might not be capable of this final revelation adds dramatic tension and underscores the profound nature of this philosophical insight. The passage ends with a cliffhanger, building anticipation for the revelation of this "single knowledge" of beauty, which will be explored in the subsequent text.

FROM 211 TO 211b

Diotima describes the ultimate goal of the lover's ascent: the vision of absolute Beauty. This Beauty is characterized by its eternal, unchanging nature, contrasting sharply with the transient beauty of physical objects. The repetitive structure emphasizes the completeness and perfection of this ideal Beauty, which transcends all particular instances of beauty.

. . .

From 211C to 211e

Diotima outlines the "ladder of love," a step-by-step process of spiritual ascent. This metaphorical ladder leads from appreciation of physical beauty to recognition of beauty in souls, laws, and knowledge, culminating in the contemplation of the Form of Beauty itself. This passage encapsulates Plato's theory of Forms, suggesting that true understanding comes from grasping universal concepts rather than particular instances.

From 212A to 212C

The text argues that the vision of true Beauty enables one to produce "true virtue" rather than mere "images of virtue." This distinction between reality and appearance is a cornerstone of Platonic philosophy. Diotima concludes by asserting that Love is humanity's greatest ally in this quest for virtue and immortality. Socrates then frames his entire speech as a eulogy to Love, underlining the central theme of the dialogue.

From 212C to 212e

The philosophical discourse is abruptly interrupted by the arrival of Alcibiades, marking a dramatic shift in the dialogue. The detailed description of Alcibiades' drunken state and elaborate attire (ivy garland, violets, ribbons) creates a vivid contrast with the lofty discussion that preceded it. This juxtaposition of the philosophical and the physical foreshadows the tension between ideal and earthly love that Alcibiades' speech will explore.

From 213A to 214e

Alcibiades' dramatic entrance marks a pivotal moment in the dialogue. His inebriated state and boisterous behavior contrast sharply with the orderly proceedings that preceded his arrival. This juxtaposition serves to highlight the Dionysian aspect of the feast, introducing an element of chaos and unpredictability to the previously Apollonian atmosphere.

The complex relationship between Alcibiades and Socrates is immediately apparent. Alcibiades' passionate declarations about Socrates reveal a mix of admiration, frustration, and desire. His claim that Socrates makes him jealous and prone to outbursts suggests a deep-seated emotional attachment, while Socrates' response indicates a more measured, perhaps even wary, attitude towards Alcibiades.

Alcibiades' insistence on heavy drinking shifts the feast's focus from intellectual discourse to a more raucous celebration. This transition reflects the Greek cultural practice of symposia, which often began with measured conversation and ended in revelry.

The setup for Alcibiades' speech about Socrates creates anticipation for a revealing and potentially scandalous account. Alcibiades' promise to speak "only the truth" suggests that his inebriated state might lead to unguarded honesty about his relationship with Socrates.

Cultural elements such as the crowning with garlands, the role of the symposiarch (toastmaster), and the large drinking vessel (psykter) provide insight into ancient Greek social customs. The reference to Homer's Iliad demonstrates the pervasive influence of epic poetry in Greek culture and education.

Plato's skillful use of dialogue and characterization brings the scene to life, offering a vivid portrayal of the interpersonal dynamics and social norms of Athenian intellectual circles.

FROM 215A TO 217e

Alcibiades' speech offers a vivid portrayal of Socrates, employing striking similes to illustrate the philosopher's character. He compares Socrates to Silenus figures and the satyr Marsyas, mythological creatures associated with wisdom and music. These comparisons emphasize Socrates' outward appearance as unattractive and rough, contrasting with his inner beauty and wisdom.

The speech highlights Socrates' unique ability to captivate his audience through words alone, surpassing even skilled orators and musicians. This power is likened to divine possession, echoing the Greek concept of enthusiasmos or divine inspiration.

Alcibiades' conflicted feelings towards Socrates reveal the philosopher's profound impact on those around him. The shame and self-reflection Socrates inspires in Alcibiades illustrate the transformative power of Socratic dialogue and its ability to challenge societal values.

The passage also touches on Greek ideals of beauty and love, particularly in the context of the erastes-eromenos relationship common in ancient Athens. Alcibiades' failed attempts to seduce Socrates subvert expectations and highlight Socrates' exceptional self-control and dedication to wisdom over physical pleasure.

Alcibiades' drunken state and his invocation of the proverb "In wine, there is truth" serve to frame his revelations as particularly honest and unguarded. This sets the stage for the more intimate revelations to follow, promising insights into Socrates' character that might otherwise remain hidden.

From 218 to 220e

Alcibiades' speech in this passage is a pivotal moment in the dialogue, revealing the complex relationship between him and Socrates. The narrative employs vivid imagery and metaphors to convey the intense emotional and intellectual impact of philosophical discourse.

Alcibiades begins with the metaphor of a viper's bite, comparing the sting of philosophical ideas to a venomous snake. This powerful imagery underscores the transformative and sometimes painful nature of philosophical inquiry, particularly for young minds encountering these ideas for the first time.

The description of the "philosophical frenzy" and "Bacchic

revelry" draws a parallel between philosophical discourse and religious ecstasy, suggesting that the pursuit of wisdom can be as intoxicating as wine. This comparison would resonate with the Greek audience familiar with Dionysian rites.

Alcibiades' attempted seduction of Socrates serves as a vehicle to illustrate Socrates' legendary self-control and dedication to wisdom over physical pleasure. The juxtaposition of Alcibiades' youthful passion with Socrates' restraint highlights the contrast between physical and intellectual forms of love, a central theme in Platonic philosophy.

The anecdotes about Socrates' behavior during military campaigns paint a picture of a man of extraordinary fortitude and self-discipline. His ability to withstand extreme cold, go without food, and remain standing in thought for an entire day and night portrays him as almost superhuman. These stories serve to elevate Socrates above ordinary men, reinforcing his status as a philosophical hero.

The reference to the expedition to Potidaea provides historical context, placing the events during the Peloponnesian War, a significant conflict between Athens and Sparta. This backdrop adds depth to the characters' experiences and relationships.

Alcibiades' admission of feeling "enslaved" by Socrates reveals the powerful effect of Socratic teaching and personality. This dynamic between student and teacher, lover and beloved, is a central theme in Platonic dialogues, exploring the nature of love, wisdom, and the pursuit of virtue.

The passage concludes with an account of Socrates' bravery in battle, saving Alcibiades' life. This act of physical courage complements Socrates' intellectual and moral strength, presenting a well-rounded portrait of the philosopher as both a thinker and a man of action.

Throughout the speech, Alcibiades addresses the other feast attendees as judges, creating a quasi-legal framework for his testimony. This rhetorical device adds gravity to his words and invites the audience (both within the dialogue and the readers) to evaluate Socrates' character based on the evidence presented.

. . .

FROM 221A TO 221C

Alcibiades begins his encomium of Socrates by recounting his behavior during military campaigns. He describes Socrates' exceptional composure and courage during the retreat from Delium, comparing him favorably to Laches, a known Athenian general. This portrayal serves to establish Socrates' physical bravery, which complements his intellectual prowess.

Alcibiades quotes Aristophanes' description of Socrates from "The Clouds," ironically using the comic poet's words to paint a heroic picture. This intertextual reference adds depth to the characterization and highlights the complex relationship between Socrates and his contemporaries.

FROM 221D TO 222A

The comparison of Socrates to sileni and satyrs is a central metaphor in Alcibiades' speech. Sileni were mythical creatures associated with Dionysus, often depicted as ugly on the outside but containing beautiful statuettes within. This analogy suggests that Socrates' outward appearance and behavior belie his inner wisdom and virtue.

Alcibiades emphasizes Socrates' unique character by stating that he is incomparable to any other person, past or present. This assertion elevates Socrates to an almost mythical status, setting him apart from even the greatest historical and legendary figures.

The description of Socrates' discussions as initially seeming ridiculous but containing profound wisdom when "opened up" is a key insight into his philosophical method. It suggests that Socrates' apparent fixation on mundane topics (pack asses, blacksmiths, etc.) is a deliberate strategy to lead his interlocutors to deeper truths.

FROM 222B TO 222E

Alcibiades' warning to Agathon about Socrates' deceptive nature in matters of love adds a layer of complexity to the praise. It reveals the personal and emotional impact Socrates has on those around him, blurring the lines between philosophical mentorship and romantic attraction.

The ensuing interaction between Socrates, Alcibiades, and Agathon demonstrates the playful yet competitive atmosphere of the feast. Socrates' clever response to Alcibiades' accusation shows his quick wit and ability to deflect personal attacks with humor.

From 223a to 223d

The concluding scene, with its chaotic influx of revelers and the gradual dispersal of guests, serves as a contrast to the structured speeches that preceded it. The image of Socrates outlasting the others in drinking and conversation reinforces his exceptional nature.

The final philosophical point about the same person being capable of writing both tragedy and comedy is a fitting conclusion to a dialogue that has blended serious philosophical discourse with humorous and dramatic elements. This idea challenges traditional distinctions between literary genres and suggests a deeper unity in the art of storytelling.

NOTES

The Feast of Eros

1. Apollodorus now begins to narrate the story as told to him by Aristodemus, shifting to a third-person perspective.
2. Heraclitus was a pre-Socratic philosopher known for his doctrine of change and unity of opposites.
3. Ate is the Greek goddess of mischief and ruin.
4. This refers to a phrase from Alcidamas, a student of the rhetorician Gorgias.
5. This quote is from an unknown source, possibly a lost work or a common saying of the time.
6. A quotation from Euripides' Hippolytus, line 612.
7. This is a reference to Homer's Iliad, Book 11, line 514.
8. This is an allusion to Homer's Iliad, where Glaucus exchanges his golden armor for Diomedes' bronze armor, getting the worse end of the deal.
9. The expedition to Potidaea was a military campaign during the Peloponnesian War, in which both Socrates and Alcibiades participated.
10. This is a reference to Aristophanes' description of Socrates in his play "The Clouds".